I WAS A TEENAGE **SEX P**ISTOL

faber and faber
———————— *review copy* ————————

-- The first account by a Sex Pistols
band member to chronicle the rise and
fall of the seminal punk rock band --

I WAS A TEENAGE SEX PISTOL

Glen Matlock
with Pete Silverton

Music
192 pages, 6 X 9
20 b&w photographs
$12.95 paperback original

Publication date: November 1991

———————— ————————

faber and faber, 50 cross street, winchester, ma 01890 (617) 721-1427
Please send us two copies of your review

I Was
A Teenage
Sex Pistol

GLEN MATLOCK
with Pete Silverton

ff
Faber and Faber
BOSTON • LONDON

First published in the United States in 1991 by Faber and Faber, Inc., 50 Cross Street, Winchester, MA 01890. First published in Great Britain in 1990 by Omnibus Press (A Division of Book Sales Limited), 8/9 Frith Street, London, W1V 5TZ.

Every effort has been made to trace the copyright holders of the photographs in this book, but one or two were unreachable. We would be grateful if the photographers concerned would contact the publishers.

Library of Congress Cataloguing-in-Publication Data

Matlock, Glen.
   I was a teenage Sex Pistol / Glen Matlock with Pete Silverton.
    p. cm.
   ISBN 0-571-12934-X (pbk.) : $12.95
    1. Sex Pistols (Musical group) 2. Rock groups—England.
   3. Matlock, Glen. I. Silverton, Pete. II. Title.
   ML421.S47M38 1991
   782.42166′092—dc20
   [B]   91-22318
                                       CIP
                                       MN

Published by arrangement with Omnibus Press (A Division of Book Sales Limited)

Cover photograph and design by Tony Foo
Back cover photograph by Bob Gruen
Picture research by Paul Giblin and Glen Matlock

Printed in the United States of America

Hey Carol...Now you know.

Contents

Introduction

Over the past decade or so, a lot of people have set themselves up as authorities on the phenomenon that came to be known as punk rock. Some of them – with tenuous links to punk rock's driving forces – have tried to come on cool and learned. In the end they have merely sounded smug – which is what happens when you theorise and philosophise your way through a movement which is quite unsuited to such an approach.

Others – those with no grasp on it at all – have portrayed it as nothing more than a fad. Here you are, they say, this was just another shallow pop movement, a here-today-gone-tomorrow fashion trend, so let's all look at the pretty pictures.

What I'm trying to do here is set the record straight, scotching the misleading stories which have so far appeared and setting out the facts as I see them. Public knowledge of The Sex Pistols' story often seems to extend no further than two episodes: we made the front pages of the British dailies by swearing on a TV show and then, a year or so later, the band fizzled out in the States where Sid Vicious was to meet his untimely death.

I take The Sex Pistols' story back to its beginnings, in West London rehearsal halls in the mid-seventies, and track the moves which culminated in our being unleashed on the Great British Public. I've concentrated on building a picture of a bunch of guys' attempts at making their way in the world that was mid-seventies London.

The general conception is that 1977 was the summer of punk, when the Roxy Club was in its heyday, when the Vortex was vorticising every night, when punks and teds were slogging it out in the Kings Road, and women's magazines demonstrated how you could achieve the punk look à la Catwoman with a packet of cheese and onion and a couple of your dad's used Gillettes. I'd like to point out that the punk's ground rules had been firmly established well before then. For me, 1976 was the summer of punk and by the end of that year the shit had truly hit the fan – the Bill Grundy show, hysterical tabloid paranoia and that rerun of the Flying Dutchman saga, the 'Anarchy' tour.

This is unashamedly the story of five people, the five men and boys who created punk rock. Steve Jones, Paul Cook, Johnny Rotten, Malcolm McLaren and myself, with a strong helping hand from Bernard Rhodes. I've tried to show each of them in an unbiased light while, at the same time, challenging any false impressions that some of them may have created with their versions of our history.

Every band member will, of course, tell a different story and I make no apology for the fact that the thoughts and views contained here are mine and mine alone. You want the other guys' opinions? Go and ask them.

What I can vouch for is the authenticity of my own tale and my contribution to the band who were the very vanguard of a movement which, to date, was the last in a line of British youth movements and which – in however small a way – actually succeeded in challenging the status quo.

My qualifications are simple. In the words of Wink Martindale: I know, I was that soldier.

Glen Matlock, London, October 1989

I WAS A TEENAGE **SEX P**ISTOL

1

The Yeti

It was all the Yeti's doing when you come right down to it. If it hadn't been for the Yeti, I'd never have met Malcolm McLaren or Johnny Rotten. Pete Dawson was his real name but no one called him that. At 15 he was six feet tall, stroke for the rowing eight, and had loads of long hair. He looked like a wild thing so we called him the Yeti.

We went to school together at St Clement Danes, an all-boys grammar school in West London, at the tail end of the period in which secondary education was split by the 11-plus into grammar schools for those who passed and secondary schools for the rest. St Clement Danes was an old-fashioned school which would have liked to have been more middle class than it was. Unfortunately, most of the kids came from the White City Estate, which is about as working class as you can get.

As well as being a mate of Yeti's at school we worked together at Whiteleys, the department store in Queensway, on Thursday evenings after school and all day Saturday for which we got paid the grand total of 36 shillings, or £1.80 today.

There was a whole gang of us who went out together at the weekends. The particular Friday night when the Yeti sealed my fate, we went to an end-of-run party for the school play,

Doctor Faustus it was that year. I'd worked on it as the slide projectionist. One of the reasons we were all so keen on going to the party was that *Faustus* was a joint production with the local girls school. When you're at an all-boys school that is really important. It's so hard to meet, let alone get off with, girls at an all-boys school.

Then, after the party, we went along to see Man at The Lyceum. It was an all-night show, the first I'd ever been to. Ace were on the bill as well. (It seemed with Ace and Man that the theme of the evening was Bands With Extremely Short Names.)

The bands started playing around 11 in the evening and, basically, people didn't go there for the music but to get a sleep if they lived too far out from central London to get home after the tubes had closed down for the night.

I remember standing at the back of The Lyceum and looking down at the crowd. It looked like a bloody great sea of Afghan coats with tufts of long hair poking out from them. (Before you ask, no, I didn't have an Afghan coat.) There was nobody dancing or even moving very much. The bar was shut. And Man were playing. They were OK in bursts but then they'd start in on one of their boring, self-indulgent, 20-minute solos. Not the most exciting of prospects maybe but even so, I was having a good time.

Then the Yeti suddenly produced all these blues – speed, amphetamine, call it what you like. The rest of my mates steamed right into them. But I didn't. Not out of any idea that taking drugs was morally wrong but simply because I was already enjoying myself and didn't feel the need of any chemical additions to that enjoyment.

I hung around The Lyceum till early morning. Then, when the show was over and it was time for everyone to wake up and go home, they opened up the roof – the whole thing rolls back to one side. It was one of those gorgeous early mornings when the sun has just risen but it's still dark enough to see the brightest stars.

We watched that for a bit, then took the first tube of the

day round to a friend's place for a while. Four or five of us were Whiteleys regulars so we all turned up there promptly for work. But I was the only one who hadn't taken the blues.

It was a very old-fashioned store – which was hardly surprising as it was the first department store in London. It certainly looked like it was. There were a couple of things that I've never seen anywhere since, relics of Victorian engineering.

The service lift was water-powered. Each time you wanted to go up or down you had to pull a chain. It was like being in a loo that rose and fell.

The cash flow was regulated by an incredibly ancient compressed air system. It must have been the last one left in London. When someone bought something you put their money and their sales docket in a little aluminum container, placing it in a tube by your counter. It would then whoosh straight off to the central cashiers' office. There, they would check it off and whoosh it back to you with the customer's change and the docket stamped. Basically, it was a late surviving example of 19th-century employers' attitudes towards their staff: checking up on them all the time or they'd have their hands in the till. It was straight out of H. G. Wells' *Mr Kipps*.

That Saturday I was fine until the afternoon. Then I began to feel totally spaced out. Everyone else – because of the blues of course – was right as nine pence. But I'd had no sleep and I was feeling it. It got worse. I was really flagging. I'd never felt that tired in my life. I started to feel quite weird.

Suddenly the Yeti turned up in the men's department where I worked. Here, Glen, he said, you won't believe what's happened. Some fucking idiot's cocking it right up. They've been putting the money into the tube and forgetting the dockets. So they're up there in the cashiers' office trying to figure out where all the money's coming from. It's total pandemonium up there.

The fucking idiot cocking it right up was yours truly, of course. I didn't hang around to take the blame, just worked that day out and sloped off home. I knew though that they'd work it out in the end so I was on the look-out for a new job.

A few days later I took a walk down the Kings Road, mostly searching for a pair of brothel creepers. I'd been after a pair for ages. I can't think why. Maybe because the teddy boy fashion was just beginning to edge back in; it was around the time of Roxy Music's Spaceman Ted look. Maybe it was because I'd seen Ronnie Lane of The Faces – who was my hero at that age – wearing a pair on TV. Something as daft as that.

There I was strolling down the scrubby end of the Kings Road, mooching along. Round the kink in the road after Beaufort Street market and there, on the right hand side, was a shop with a pair of creepers in the window.

Let It Rock, it was called. Or maybe Too Fast To Live, Too Young To Die. It had signs up for both so I never could work out which it was.

I walked inside and it was just like my granny's sitting room. Not only did it sell teddy boy clothes but there was also a fifties radiogram and fifties wallpaper. It was all put together with really good attention to detail.

Straightaway I thought: I need a job and this really looks like somewhere interesting to work. As soon as I set foot in there, I knew that I had to be involved somehow. So I asked them if they needed anyone to help out on Saturdays. The guy behind the counter said, we do as it happens but you'll have to speak to Malcolm when he comes in.

Eventually this bloke turned up, the one he'd called Malcolm. He was wearing some kind of rock 'n' roll suit, the sort of thing that Jerry Lee Lewis might have worn – or more likely the duds you'd see on a young country buck in one of those dreadful fifties US musicals like *Carousel* or *County Fair*.

It was flecked cloth with zips down the side of the jacket – which looked absolutely horrible – and peg trousers. At that time no one was wearing peg trousers. He was selling teddy boy gear but what he was wearing – drecky as it was – had moved on beyond that into something new.

Before I even had a chance to talk to him he was all round

the shop talking to everyone. The strange thing was that he spoke to everybody with a different accent. Sometimes posh, sometimes American. What's up with this bloke? I thought. He can't seem to make up his mind who he is. By the time he got to me his accent was thick Cockney, all 'cor blimey'. He sounded like my grandad actually.

'Ere, what you bin doin' then, boy? he said.

Working at Whiteleys.

Whiteleys, eh? That's where Brian Jones worked. What else do you do?

I'm at school.

Why do you want to work here?

Well, I need a job. And, as soon as I'd said that, I realised it was the wrong thing to have said.

What do you mean? he asked suspiciously.

Forget it, I said. For a moment I thought he was going to tell me to sling my hook. Then he must have changed his mind. Well, we do need someone, he said.

And that was that. I was Malcolm McLaren's Saturday lad. It wasn't that I was an amazing person or exactly the right guy for the job. It was just that I happened to ask at the right moment. They needed someone and I turned up asking. The right face at the right time.

The bonus for me was that the money was so much better than Whiteleys. Instead of getting 36 bob for Thursday evening and all day Saturday, Malcolm paid me three pounds 10 shillings – almost twice as much – for the Saturday only. Plus, while I had to get up at eight for Whiteleys, I didn't have to get into Let It Rock until 11. So I was well happy.

When I first started there I really felt like the proverbial spare prick at a wedding. I turned up dressed in what I thought were my best clothes – a corduroy suit from Take Six with Oxford bags à la Trevor Eve in *Shabby Tiger*, which was on TV at the time. Both of which were quite cool things to wear then. Certainly nobody else at my school was wearing anything like that. They were all into loon pants or being heavy

7

duty skinheads. But Malcolm's shop was light years away from anything I'd seen or known.

The first day there I noticed all these queens waltzing in and out. New experience for me, boy. But I got talking to one of them and he told me he'd just come out of prison where he'd done time for soliciting. Blimey, I said, it must have been pretty heavy for you in there.

Oooh no, dear, he said. All those rough men. I loved it.

Quite an eye-opener for a 15-year-old grammar school boy from Kensal Green.

My parents called me Glen after the bandleader who took one too many cross-channel flights. Swing was the music they'd grown up with and courted to. So my name was a kind of tribute to their courtship.

My dad was a coach builder and my mum worked at the gas board. We were never poor but it was no life of suburban luxury. Respectable working class, that's the phrase they use about families like mine. Reasonable jobs, best suit on Sundays and parlours as clean as operating rooms.

We had never moved, always living in the same place: 18 Ravensworth Road, Kensal Green. A late Victorian artisan's house it was, a two-up-two-down with me and my parents on the top floor. Bathtime meant filling a hot tin tub from kettles.

Downstairs in the other two rooms lived an Irish family. We were always having rows with them about the back garden, territorial disputes over 15-square-feet of packed mud covered in cat shit. My mother really looked down on them. You know, she'd say, they cook their cabbage in the same water as the bacon.

Then, when I was 14, my dad bought the house. Suddenly we had four rooms, a plumbed in bath and no poor Irish downstairs.

Kensal Green then was an old-fashioned, tight-knit working class community, the kind that had survived through thick and thin since Victoria was on the throne and that nowadays only exists in sociology textbooks and TV soaps. A lot of our family lived in the same road. Both my nan and my uncle Colin, my mum's brother, lived at number 28.

Them aside, though, it was a small family. Not only was I an only child but my dad's father was an orphan and my mum's family had been happy to get out of Kensal Town—which was a little down the road. A real heavy duty place it was in those days.

As I grew up in Kensal Green—which is just up the road from Ladbroke Grove—it became one of the areas the first wave of black immigrants came to. Lots of West Indians. Walk down the street and there was always Blue Beat coming out of a window.

We used to play football in the streets with the lead singer of The Skatalites—when we could entice him out. I can't remember his name but he was something of a latecomer to the band. They'd had their one hit with 'Guns Of Navarone' and he was the toaster by the time they were doing the small-time club circuit.

He lived in my mate Densil Alleyne's house. Densil's mum let him a room. We'd shout up from the street to him. Hey, coming out to play football? We never seemed to see anything strange in the fact that he was maybe 10 years older than us. Alright, he'd shout back, soon as I'm finished with these two women now. He'd have these two hideous, fat, white women up there and when he'd finished he'd come down to play football in the street. Always barefoot and with real hipster trousers which showed the cheeks of his bum.

It was a poor area. Nobody had a flash car. The best you saw were third-hand Morris Minors or—as we called them—Wogmobiles, Mark Two Zodiacs or Zephyrs with every conceivable extra. Sun visors, whitewall tyres, furry dice hanging from the mirror, umpteen fog lamps, whiplash aerials, the whole bit. Self-cleaning oven, so far as I knew.

There was no major racial tension around but there was always a slight twist on the relationship with black people. I was a little bit of a skinhead myself for a while. I had the Sta Prest and the short hair, and every party you went to it would be all Tamla and Blue Beat and ska.

But, although I heard that music, I never saw it as the kind of music I'd be involved in. And that was because Kensal Green was a deprived place and the most deprived people were the blacks. Terrible as it sounds, you didn't want to be associated with that deprivation. It was a downer. You wanted out. There was no question of not liking blacks, it was a question of social standing. If you wanted some, that wasn't the avenue to go down.

It had nothing to do with friendships though. Phil Fearon, the soul singer, went to junior school with me. I remember we all went on a school trip to the Geffrye Museum of period furniture and costume in Hackney, East London. They showed us a spinette and asked if anyone could play the piano. Phil stepped right up and tinkled out 'Danger Man' and the theme from *Robinson Crusoe*. (Years later, he came down to a jam with The Pistols when I thought we needed a keyboard player. There was a funny atmosphere all the time he was there. Then, after he'd left, the other guys turned to me and said, what you doing bringing a sooty down?)

Another thing that cut me off from the other kids was going to the grammar school and having to wear a bright green blazer every day. There were quite a few Asian kids at the school but very few blacks—particularly few when you consider how black West London is.

Mikey Craig, from Culture Club, was one of the few. I used to play football with him. Speedy Matlock, they used to call me. I played fullback, tearing up the wing—a right clogger, always kicking people in the air.

In fact, it was something of a school for bass players. Not only was there Mikey and myself but in the year above me was Gary Fraser, brother of Free's Andy Fraser, who played in Stray. (The rest of Stray went to Christopher Wren—Steve and Paul's alma mater.)

That was the London of my childhood and youth. A London that was still, 20 years after the event, recovering from the Second World War. There were bomb sites around and a lot of it looked like something out of the Ealing comedies.

But this wasn't the London most people think of. Mine wasn't the city of sophisticated, cosmopolitan life. In some ways I might as well have been in the Outer Hebrides. Now everyone's got a car it's difficult to explain how isolated somewhere like Kensal Green used to be in those days.

It was a world unto itself, a working class community that existed quite separately from central London—which we thought of as Town, a totally different place. It was only a few miles away but it seemed unimaginably distant. Even Whiteleys. That was at most a couple of miles up the road and no more than a few pence on the bus. But to go there was to enter another world.

And Malcolm's shop, that was another universe.

2

Blind Lemon
Matlock

apart from liking London bands such as The Stones and The Kinks, for some reason I always had a working knowledge of The Small Faces. I remember seeing them on *Ready Steady Go* and liking Ronnie Lane's smile. Although I was really young, I was struck by his attitude. All bands smiled when they were on TV then. But, while pop bands like The Tremeloes and The Searchers seemed to be smiling just because they were on TV and feeling famous, The Small Faces had much cooler smiles.

Their smiles were like a knowing wink: sussed and streetwise without being in the least dour or po-faced. I cottoned on to that. It wasn't so much a case of thinking: he looks a lovely chappie. It was more: now there's a cheeky chappie.

After that I went off music for a while. Then one evening – I must have been 12 or 13 at the time – we were driving back from visiting my nan. The car was an old Morris Minor. It didn't even have a radio fitted. So we used to take a big old transistor with us and put it on the back shelf. Every time the car went round a corner you had to turn the whole radio round to face a different way. That was the only way you could get half-decent reception.

I was sitting there looking out of the window and suddenly

this wonderful record came on. It was 'The Israelites' by Desmond Dekker. I kept on listening to the show. It turned out to be the Mike Raven programme on Radio One. He'd play all kinds of black music, everything from ska to soul and blues.

Strangely enough, I got into the blues. He played one record I liked so much I decided to go out and buy it. It was by Blind Lemon Jefferson. A 13-year-old white kid living in Kensal Green going out to buy a Blind Lemon Jefferson album, I ask you!

The mates that I played football with were skinheads into Blue Beat while the girls were into that pop group The Love Affair. They all went to the local comprehensive – which I *wanted* to but, because I passed my 11-plus, I got sent to the grammar instead. That made me feel a bit of an outsider. That bright green blazer we had to wear didn't help much either.

So, I suppose going out to buy Blind Lemon Jefferson was a deliberate search for something esoteric. It was like finding my own identity by finding something different to like, something different to what all my friends liked.

But they didn't have the Blind Lemon album in the shop. How about this instead? said the guy, showing me 'The Story Of The Blues'. It had 'Parchman Farm' on it – country blues stuff and city blues from the thirties like 'Butterbeans' and 'Susie'. But it also went right up to the fifties. Elmore James and Otis Spann, things like that. I thought, hang on, this is more like it.

So I became the only bluesman in Kensal Green. I already had a guitar. 'Guaranteed Not To Split', it said on it – which was just as well as much later I had the initial idea for 'Anarchy' while messing around on it. I'd been given it when I was seven but I'd never learnt to play it. Now I had the blues and playing it was suddenly all so easy.

The blues really are elementary. Three chords and you could play just about anything on the album. I'd sit up in my room bashing out the blues like I was Blind Lemon Matlock. Then, when I got fed up with that, I'd go downstairs and make a racket on the old upright piano my nan had lent us.

14

A lot of blokes say the reason they got into music in the first place was they thought it would be a great way of pulling women. All those girls in the front row, that kind of thing.

But I reckon that's bravado on their part. Most people in bands have quite similar backgrounds and I reckon a lot of them shared the same experience as I did. And that idea never came into it.

Mostly, it was just a way of keeping myself occupied. Going to grammar school really made me isolated. It was only a couple of miles away from where I lived, but that's a long way when you're only 11 years old and all your mates from junior school had gone to the local comprehensive round the corner.

Not only that – they also thought, because I'd gone to the grammar, that suddenly I was too snooty to be friends with them. And, on top of that, all the new friends I made at the grammar lived out West, in Greenford or Ealing.

So, through no fault of my own, I was at a loose end quite a bit. I felt ostracised quite honestly. Starting to play music was a way round that. It was a way of entertaining myself, passing the time. No big mission, no feeling that I was going to change the world with my music. That came later.

Around then I also got hold of a folk album by Pete Seeger and I remember being really struck by a track called 'Goofing Off Suite'. I dug the idea of being free enough to just goof off from incessant math homework.

Eventually I moved on from the blues, picking up on Ronnie Lane again, only by this time The Small Faces had become The Faces. So, impressed by him, I got myself a bass guitar. Which was absolutely stupid. There is nothing worse than playing a bass guitar – without an amp because you can't afford one yet – all on your jack up in your bedroom.

The bass I had was awful as well. A Rossetti. I haven't seen one since. The jack plug was soldered on – which meant you couldn't pull the lead out, you had to wrap the plug and lead around the neck before you could put it away. For me that meant wrapping it in a blue launderette bag which served as a case.

Some time later I got an amp as well. It was as big a piece of junk as the bass – a Fenton Weill Mk II with a Goodman speaker, which is nothing but a cheap copy of the Ampeg Portaflex B15N. (I sold it eventually – for 15 quid. I was going on the school trip to the Norfolk Broads and needed some spending money.)

But, playing through the amp, I began to realise how daft it was sitting up in my bedroom by myself with it, trying to work my way through tunes. I'm going to have to start playing with other people, I thought.

So I got together with a couple of blokes from school. 'Hold Your Head Up' by Argent was in the charts at the time. We'd play that again and again and again. It was the only bass line I could play properly – because it's so simple; it's exactly the same all the way through.

We'd rehearse in the huts after school, having squared it with the music teacher. The singer, Steve Mariner, was a bloke in the choir with a really high voice who thought he was Jack The Lad. You weren't allowed to smoke on school premises but he'd always light up while we were rehearsing.

One day, the head of sixth form – a teacher called Don Palmer – came in and asked what we were doing. He was obviously peeved that we'd squared it with the music teacher while he didn't know anything about it. Anyway, Jack The Lad said, rehearsing, and blew smoke in his face. The next day we were informed that we weren't allowed to use the huts again. Jack The Lad, of course, was right in the shit for smoking on school premises. And that was the end of that band.

Except some time later there was a school dance. Don Palmer asked if our band would play at it. No, we said. Why? We're just not good enough, we had nowhere to rehearse, you see. That was basically spite, of course, but you always start as you mean to go on.

It was an odd period in music. It was the time of progressive rock. Led Zeppelin and Jethro Tull were meant to be a more intelligent kind of music which appealed to sixth formers, like me. But they all looked like complete prats.

On the other hand, T. Rex might have looked really good but everything else about them was so naïve and teenybopperish that you couldn't really admit to your mates that you liked them.

There just wasn't much British around that had an edge and at the same time looked good. Just The Faces, maybe Slade and then Bowie, really.

The biggest impact Bowie had on me was with his haircut. I thought it was really something new. I had shortish hair at the time. Like all schools then, mine had a rule about long hair. You were only allowed to have it down to just below the bottom of your ears, which looked absolutely daft. I'd had enough of my hair looking like a toilet brush, so I always had it cut short – like Ronnie Lane's, of course – which was less hassle.

Then came Bowie. Straightaway I went off and had a bright red flash put in across the front of my hair. When I got home my dad took one look at it and said, you look like a bleeding nancy boy. He didn't talk to me for a week after that.

The next day in school all my mates started calling me Ginger. Then came Pure Maths – with Don Palmer. Not only had I had that run in with him over the rehearsals, but he was also the fussiest teacher in the school when it came to long hair. He stood there writing on the blackboard. Then every now and again he'd turn round and stare at me, his mouth open, totally incredulous. You could see his brain working. I must be able to do something about this, he was thinking, but there was no rule against hair colour, only length. I loved that, seeing him stuck for words. It was like: gotcha.

I did my 'O' levels, and then my 'A's, but really I had no particular academic drive. I never wanted to go to university although I do know that my mum and dad always had it in the back of their minds that I would go.

But nor did I want to go out to work. From somewhere I got the idea of going to art college. I'm sure it was because I'd read about all the rock musicians who'd started their bands at art colleges – John Lennon and Keith Richards in particular.

I was interested in drawing but I never saw it as part of a potential career. I went to art college for the music not for the art. In fact, I only became a half decent painter after I got into art college.

3

Let It **R**ock

the particular premises that Let It Rock occupied had always been in the very vanguard of London fashion trends but working there wasn't as much of a shock as I thought it was going to be at first. The way people looked was the most shocking thing. They were all so done up and seemed so aloof. Yet, in fact, they were really easygoing and fine to get along with.

I'm thinking of people like Jean Krell, who owned Granny Takes A Trip, the painter Humphrey Ocean and Bernard Rhodes, the friend of Malcolm's who went on to manage The Clash. They all came from similar backgrounds and, as like minds, they were all congregating at the same place for the same reasons.

They all used to hang out there and quite a scene developed. Some of it had to do with it being the antithesis of the whole trash/sleaze thing that was going down at the start of the seventies. Cockney Rebel had it a bit, and it was the time of the film *Cabaret*, *The Rocky Horror Show* and Biba's nightclub on the roof of what used to be Derry and Toms. Every other phrase in the newspapers seemed to be 'lounge lizard'. The cover of Bryan Ferry's second solo album – with him in a white tuxedo by a swimming pool – really sealed it.

That was what was supposedly chic. Personally I thought it was a load of fucking cobblers and yet that was the swamp from which punk rock emerged.

You could tell that the real reason people came into the shop was to hang out. Bernard Rhodes, for example, was always in the shop and he was always up for a chat. I talked to him a lot and we struck up a rapport.

Bernie was seen as a bit of an oddball – although not by me – but he was very instrumental in getting The Pistols together, especially when Malcolm was away. They'd been friends for some time when I first knew them but I didn't realise how long. Bernie would always have it that he had known Malcolm since he was a mod in the sixties hanging out at – among other places – Eel Pie Island, where The Who and The Stones used to play.

I didn't believe him at first. I thought he was having us on, exaggerating – because there were always people hanging out, trying to crash Malcolm's scene. But this time, it turns out he was telling the truth. His line was that he'd lost contact with Malcolm because he could only stand to be with him for so long at a stretch. Then he'd have to go off and do something else for a while before he could stomach being with him again. They were like Little And Large in a way, but I never did work out which one was the straight man.

Bernie did one very important thing for The Pistols. He made us focus our thoughts. In the early days of the band, before John arrived, he'd beaver away at us in the pub, making us think through our attitudes. We'd be sitting there talking about music and he'd dive in. Fucking hell, he'd say, you don't really like The Faces, do you? Why? And you'd have to think about it, then tell him. But that was never enough. Well then, he'd say, what *don't* you like about them? Well, Rod Stewart, he's a bit of a cunt. Why is he a cunt? Bernie would go on and on at you like that, making you define and redefine your attitudes.

I remember having some really interesting discussions with him when we'd go and see a band somewhere. All of us

20

were checking new bands out the whole time. For two reasons. One, like any new band we were checking out the opposition. Two, it was a strange time. There was a rock 'n' roll vacuum. We were looking for anybody who could help fill it. There was almost a desperation about the way we'd try and fill our recreational time with something worthwhile.

There was always pub rock, in sweaty drinkers like The Kensington in Torrington, The Hope And Anchor, The Greyhound and The Nashville. Mostly they were second-rate copies of the kind of American bar-room R&B bands the members of these pub bands had seen in the days when they had a bit more going for them and had actually made it to the States one time in the late sixties or early seventies.

For the price of a pint, you could catch Bees Make Honey, Ducks Deluxe, The Tyla Gang or Brinsley Schwarz. And many a night I spent at The Greyhound watching Brinsley Schwarz, diligently studying Nick Lowe's bass playing. However, aside from the fact that their musicianship was pretty solid, these pub bands were still really mundane to a young kid looking further ahead.

Later there were bands like The Vibrators, The Stranglers and The Hammersmith Gorillas, horrors one and all, but pride of place in the pub rock pantheon went to Wilko Johnson's Dr Feelgood and the wonderfully esoteric Kilburn And The High Roads, featuring Ian Dury and kitted out courtesy of Let It Rock.

We were always out there looking for something new, trying to find any slight glimmer of someone with the same kind of ideas as us. We'd go right out of our way in the search. Once Bernie and I dragged right across town to a pub in the back of beyond in North London because we'd seen a gig advertised there featuring a band called The Teenage Rebels.

They were absolute rubbish. They had no idea. They were on a totally different wavelength from us. We went looking for like minds and found aliens.

Bernie went up to the singer after the show and said, we

thought you were called The Teenage Rebels, yet you're not teenagers and you're certainly not rebellious.

That's the point, said the singer, we're rebelling against teenagers.

Bernie was speechless, for the first time since I'd known him. Yet another wasted exercise, we thought.

Sometimes when we'd been out to clubs Bernie would give me a lift home to my parents', out in Greenford where we'd moved just about the time I started keeping twilight hours. Which was a right drag – Kensal Green was a quid cab ride from the West End, which was within my pocket. But Greenford was in Middlesex and many was the night I spent in the pissing rain having walked to Acton Town station to wait for the first train home in the morning. And we'd sit there in the car for an hour or so, chatting through what we were trying to do. It was like some kind of School Of Rock 'n' Roll.

Cor blimey, Bernie, I said, you're just like my teacher. I was half-joking, half-serious. But he clammed up right after that.

If Bernie hadn't been around we would have been a band, and we would have been a good band, but we wouldn't have been *the* band. He had a real ability for making people decide exactly what they were trying to say and do.

He put it all into practice with The Clash. When he got Joe Strummer into The Clash, he asked me what I thought of him. He's alright, I said, but he's a bit old. Don't you worry about that, said Bernie, I'll have 10 years off him. And he was right, he did. Next time I saw Joe he looked maybe not 10 years younger but certainly a totally different man and ready to rock.

What Bernie gave The Clash and us was an understanding of the importance of being clear-cut. If you are, it's a real strength. It's like going to buy a packet of peas: you know exactly which brand you want, you go right to it without dithering around.

Now this emphasis on focusing and honing everything right down to its simplest form can sound a bit like naked capitalism, treating rock 'n' roll as nothing more than a game.

But, if you want to be a success, that's what you have to do. You have to be really clear-cut about who you are and what you're trying to achieve. Bernie was wonderful at making us think all that through.

The shop was the hip place to hang out. It was the temple for everyone who wanted to be involved in something that had nothing to do with what most people thought was 'happening' in that part of the seventies. It was a world away from both glam rock and the soul boy look.

It was a place for people who wanted to stick their necks out. Lots of people are fed up with the way their lives are headed but they don't often take the trouble to do anything about it. Most of them just go with the flow, ending up as something like a gas fitter or a policeman. Not that I have anything against gas fitters, but I do think that to do what I did at 16 takes a bit more courage.

At that age everybody is down on you. Your friends, your parents, your school, your peers, they all try and stop you going out into left field. It's not a big deal in the scheme of things but you get an awful lot of hassle when all your mates are going to university, or start bringing home the bacon.

Meanwhile, you don't feel that way inclined. Suddenly it seems that only certain avenues are considered as suitable options for you. So you're kicking against the pricks right from the start.

Just by opting for a more left field occupation you're putting yourself on the edge a bit. It really does take a bit of bottle to do that and find your own way through the maze rather than just go with the flow. All of which inevitably makes you more forward-looking.

Surprisingly, working in Malcolm's shop made me feel quite at home. Not because I actually felt at home with all the 'weirdos' in there but because the shop really did look like my nan's house.

And that meant a lot to me at the time because all the paintings I was doing were subjects from my childhood years.

Not because I wanted to go back to my childhood but because I had a deep, healthy interest in finding out a bit more about what was happening while I was growing up.

As a film like *Scandal* might make young people go back and check out more about what was happening in the early sixties, so I was doing the same in terms of the fifties.

I was really into checking out fifties style. The general idea of the clothes was pretty well known: this was when Malcolm was selling updated versions of teddy boy clothes from the fifties. When I started in the shop I was into digging out a bit more detail about it, finding out the kind of Arthur English-style kipper ties my grandad used to wear and the cars that were around then.

For example, I really liked the Jowett Javelin but by then they'd already pretty much disappeared. About the only place you could see them was on the scrap heap. So the very few that were still on the road I really treasured and appreciated seeing. I was interested in all this for the simple reason that as something that takes your fancy passes you, you only get a glimpse. Then, when you get the chance, you want to have a closer look and check it out.

Let It Rock did unbelievably good business. Friday night or Saturday morning a lorry would turn up with a delivery of creepers – the very things that enticed me into the shop in the first place. We'd stock up the shelves and by the middle of the afternoon all that would be left would be size 14s in puce and some size fives that maybe a girl would pop in and buy for a party just before we shut.

A lot of money was generated by *that*, I know. Tommy Roberts used to phone me on a Saturday when I first started working there. He'd been the man behind Mr Freedom, the shop that was the first place to sell T-shirts with slogans printed on them. Nik Cohn, the writer, described him as, 'an amiable fatman from Catford, a bit of a slag and conspicuously so but shrewd, funny and hard to dislike.' I can't improve on that.

At the time he'd just started City Lights, a new shop in Covent Garden. This was well before it became a tourist attraction, when it was still a fruit and veg market. Tommy's always been one step ahead. Often one step too many for his own good. He managed Ian Dury before Dury was famous, and City Lights provided the suit that David Bowie wore on the cover of *Pin-Ups* and which people were forever coming into Let It Rock trying to get copied, much to Malcolm's chagrin. Tommy'd ask me how much money we'd done that day. I was the Saturday lad, he was a mate of Malcolm's, what did I know? So I'd tell him. It was a grand or more each time.

Eventually Malcolm realised I was telling Tommy and put me wise about how sly fat slags from Catford can be. Next time Tommy asked I kept my mouth shut.

Malcolm also slowly moved into made-to-measure tailoring, probably because of teddy boys coming in and asking for stuff to be made up. Then he moved on from that, into what he called Alan Ladd suits.

They were pretty much the style of suits that people wear now – double-breasted with peg trousers – but then they were something of a revolution. Like most of the clothes Malcolm sold they were beautifully made, of pale coloured gabardine. I always really wanted one but the trouble was they were 70 quid a pop, which I certainly couldn't afford on a Saturday lad's money – even the Saturday lad's money that Malcolm paid.

Another line was what he called his jazz suits. They were made of City Gent-type striped cloth and had even more violently pegged trousers. The jacket was very fitted and single-breasted, cutting in sharp at the waist – which made the trousers balloon right out.

It looked like something you might see in a photograph of black New Orleans in the thirties. (Which is probably exactly where Malcolm got the idea from.) It was nothing really radical in terms of modern design – even apart from Malcolm having adapted it from a picture – but it had great presence. Like an awful lot of other things Malcolm worked on.

This is where I was first introduced to Paul Cook and Steve Jones, both of whom were regulars in the shop. They'd get off the bus from West London there because they were such big Faces fans and Malcolm's shop was right next door to the home of the dandy fashion shop Granny Takes A Trip—a shop which had a Cadillac sticking out of its window—where The Faces and The Stones bought their clothes.

Steve was a new face to me but Paul I already knew from playing football against him down at the Lillie Road recreation ground. There was a little five-a-side league there. He was a good footballer and he always looked a bit weird with his striking blond hair. However, there was something of a monkey-like mischievous-ness about him.

Whenever they came into the shop Steve'd be on about: where's the action? Bernie got absolutely sick of him. Blimey, he said, if that bloke asks where the action is one more time I really don't know what I'll do. If we knew where the action was, do you think we'd be sitting around here?

I knew they had a band because Malcolm would talk to them about it. How's it going? he asked one day.

Blinking Del, they said. Del was Paul's brother-in-law and supposed to be their bass player. He hardly ever turned up though and when he did—despite being married to Paul's sister —he'd bring girls with him to bolster his ego. Now he was someone whose only real interest in pop music was the girls in the front row.

Del just had to go, they told Malcolm. We've got to find a new bass player.

Coincidentally I'd just told Malcolm that I was a bass player—although at this point I was only mucking around by myself at home—so Malcolm told them. It was as simple as if they'd asked him if he knew a good plumber. Again, right face, right time.

We happened to meet up that very night, at The Marquee where we'd all gone to see Thin Lizzy. Fancy a try-out with us? they said.

Okay.

Then come down to Wally's tomorrow afternoon.

Wally's real name was Warwick Nightingale, resident of

Hemlock Road, East Acton. He had a Rod Stewart haircut, feather cut and shaggy, and mostly he'd dress in Granny Takes A Trip kind of clothes with maybe one thing added from Malcolm's shop, a pair of creepers perhaps. He had the most disgusting rotten teeth and horn rim glasses with milk bottle lenses. On a good day he looked like a mixture of Rod Stewart, Steve Jones and Buddy Holly.

He went to the same school as Steve and Paul, Christopher Wren. One of the reasons they all became friends was that Wally's mum and dad didn't mind that he bunked off school all the time. Paul's house was always full of people and Steve didn't really have a home at all – when his mum remarried, his stepfather couldn't stand him and didn't want him around.

So, as far as I can work it out, they found it was cool to go round to Wally's and hang out, particularly as the school was only just round the corner from his place. So they'd sit there doing very little and getting bored.

But, of course, the devil finds work for idle hands, and they began thieving, acquiring all manner of things but particularly musical equipment. When they realised it was mostly too hot to sell they thought maybe it wasn't such a bad idea to learn how to play.

Paul took up the drums, Steve sang and Wally became a guitarist, not a bad one either, very much in the Ron Wood school.

As they were so into The Faces, they'd go down to Richmond, to Sir John Mills' old house, which Ron Wood had just bought. Keith Richards used to stay in the little cottage at the bottom of Ron's garden. Steve and others would get in there, rifle around it, have a go on one of Keith's guitars, nick a shirt and leave a little note saying, 'Steve was here.' That was their fun of a Saturday night.

Wally was an odd bloke though. I always thought he fancied himself as a bit like a character in a war film, *The Dambusters* – Bomber Harris, maybe. He was like the bloke who you saw right through the film overseeing the whole operation, just standing there sticking little pins into a map. I could never really work out the basis of his friendship with Steve and Paul. They were pretty street-wise while he was just odd. Strange bedfellows.

But his parents' place in Hemlock Road was their base for a long time. They'd go round there and have meetings over cups of tea. It was there I first auditioned for the band.

Wally's dad, who was always popping in asking if anyone wanted to come down the pub – he was always off to the pub – also wrote the lyrics to our first song, 'Scarface'. They were truly horrendous: 'Scarface, scarface, scarred from ear to ear, Scarface, the girls don't even care.' Terrible.

We knew they had to go so we messed around with it. In time to come, John would add some new words, all about a girl he knew who kept trying to commit suicide: 'Blood on the ceiling, blood on the walls, blood on the floor.'

That wasn't the ticket either. Finally Paul came up with an idea, 'Did You No Wrong'. But we stuck with the same tune that Wally had come up with. If you listen to 'Did You No Wrong', you can hear The Faces influence.

It's a real Ron Wood lick, which is what Wally was all about. In those early days we were a real sub-Faces band, all Gibson guitars and plonking bass lines. That was the common ground between us; the reason I got the job in the first place was because I could play The Faces' 'Three Button Hand Me Down'.

Wally was in the band a couple of years. It was during that time we all learned to play properly. It took a hell of a long time but learn we did.

The line-up was Paul on drums, me on bass, Wally on guitar and Steve singing. Later on Steve got – what do I mean got, he stole it – another guitar and started playing as well as singing. Gradually his playing became better than his singing.

The very first proper rehearsal I had with them was in the Covent Garden Community Centre. Wally's dad was there, pissed as usual. In fact, when he drove us home he was in such a state I had to get out of the van. As we walked down towards the community centre they all stopped off somewhere to steal some cymbals. I thought, fucking Ada, who are this crowd?

After that we spent a lot of time practising in what later became Riverside Studios. They belonged to Hammersmith Council who had bought them from the BBC for something like three million pounds. Wally's dad had the contract to clear them out, sort out what could be sold off and junk the rest.

He gave us a set of keys and we started going there regularly, setting it up nicely. Paul was an apprentice electrician at Watneys brewery in Mortlake so he brought some barrels of beer along and we set up a proper bar.

It was a wonderful studio as well. It had one of the best acoustic sound-dubbing rooms in Europe – they'd been fitted out some time in the thirties to be used for putting soundtracks onto movies. When Steve and Paul brought in all their stolen gear, it looked like a right little Aladdin's cave.

It was down at Riverside that I had what you might call my first 'exotic' sexual experience. Up until then I was still pretty naïve when it came to affairs of the heart. The woman was older than me, a certain rock star's girlfriend, an American who was in the shop all the time, obviously at a bit of a loose end while her boyfriend was touring.

One day in the shop she'd been waiting for Malcolm's girlfriend and partner, Vivienne Westwood – they'd been planning to go somewhere but Vivienne hadn't turned up, she'd phoned to tell this American girl that. When she was on the phone to Vivienne she suddenly turned round and shouted, which one's Glen?

Me, why?

Vivienne said I should hang out with you for a while and then we can meet up with Malcolm later.

She came down to Riverside with me, watched as we rehearsed, then followed me into the loo and gave me a blowjob – something I just wasn't used to as a 17-year-old grammar school boy still living at home with his mum and dad. Then I went back to rehearsing with the band while she sat around listening.

When it was over we all squeezed into Steve's van and drove up to Dingwalls, the club in Camden. It was a little Mini van that he ran around in, saying it was for the band but really he had it because he thought it was 'a good shagging mobile' with just enough space in the back for 'entertaining'.

She never managed to meet up with Vivienne and, as there didn't seem to be much happening at Dingwalls, we decided to drive down to Brighton, all of us crammed into the back of the Mini van. There was me and her, Wally, Malcolm and Paul.

Of course, when we got to Brighton there was nothing going on there either. So we ended up staying the night at a hotel, The Majestic, the big one right on the sea front. As usual Malcolm feigned being borassic so she ended up shelling out for two rooms. Steve, Paul, Malcolm and Wally had one. She and I had the other.

When we got to the room she went to pull the curtains. Don't bother, I said, it's six floors up. All that's out there is sea. No one can see in.

So we went to bed. Everything was fine except that when we were at it I did hear these funny noises coming from somewhere. As I couldn't work out where they were coming from I ignored them.

Then, the next morning, Steve started giving me a pep talk, all this advice on how to fuck. Don't do it like that, he said, do it like this. I know, believe me, and you're doing it all wrong.

So, Mr Knowitall, I said, how do you know?

Because, he said, I had a look at you last night, didn't I.

It turned out that he'd inched along the parapet – a thin one about six inches wide – and had a good peek at us through the windows. He was probably fed up with having to sleep four to a bed.

For a bit of fun before we went back to London we got a boat trip round the harbour. Then, in the van on the way back, the American girl noticed Malcolm yawning.

Feeling tired? she said.

Yeah, he said. You don't sleep too well four to a bed.

So she pulled out a rolled up tenner and a small packet. Here, she said, I've got some Charlie left.

Malcolm opened it up. But there was nothing there. The spray on the boat had got to it, more or less dissolving it all away.

After that I saw her maybe a couple of times. I guess, looking back on it, I was her toy boy. She was about 10 years older than me. But nothing much came of it.

In fact, I gave her the bum's rush – although it was quite inadvertent. A couple of weeks after Brighton she came into the shop, presuming we were going out together that evening – without having told me what she intended. I'd arranged to go and see a band with a mate from art college.

Bye, I said to her, got to go now.

I'd not been thinking of us as boyfriend and girlfriend, you see. But one look at her face told me she had.

4

Sex

Suddenly Malcolm decided to change everything about the shop—name, stock, attitude. It was to be Sex. Fetishism. Rubber clothes. Things that no other fashion shop would dare sell. What sparked the idea off, I really don't know. I'm sure Malcolm and Vivienne had discussions but, at that stage, I was just the Saturday lad. They didn't make me part of their discussions.

Later I thought it through and decided a big part of it was that, although Malcolm was coining it from the teds, I think he felt he was seen by his peers as an artistic cretin. All he was doing was catering to one particularly backward-looking group of people.

He and Vivienne were also probably fed up with the teds' meathead mentality. Basically, they were forerunners of the skinhead attitudes which re-emerged in the mid-seventies. They had the same right wing, racist, hard-nut minds. A bit more cultured, a bit more refined, a bit more genteel. But they would kick your head in if you spilt their pint, just the same.

They got fed up with that. I think Malcolm saw it as a way of getting himself established, starting a shop and making a reputation. But now it was time to move on. Time for a change.

The first I knew about it was Malcolm going on about rubber. This was around the time he first started seeing me as more than just an employee. Once he'd found out that I was applying to go to art school he opened up quite a bit and we began to talk.

We're going to change this shop into Sex, he said. Yeah, we're going to have these rubber clothes. Maybe masks with zips in.

He had all these old catalogues from Soho sex shops which he'd go through, things like *She And Me*, pointing out what he was going to do.

Sex itself was a strong idea but it evolved quite slowly. Malcolm wanted to create the most direct statement of what clothes were about. OK, he said, all clothes are basically a way of attracting the opposite sex. So let's go with that.

It's debatable whether that statement is true, but it was certainly pretty blatant. As he realised it would, it had the impact of blatancy. It was shocking and it brought him even more public and media attention.

But it pissed me off no end when he finally decided to change over because he shut up shop while he did it, leaving me with no Saturday job and no money. So I used to call up quite regularly, asking how the refit was going. Ar, boy, he'd say, nothing's happening yet. Give us a call next week.

Finally, he got so used to me calling that he asked me to come down and give them a hand fixing it up. I helped do the Sex sign and put all this foam rubber on the walls, which were then decorated with quotations from Alexand Trocchi, soft porn spray can graffiti from the '68 Paris student revolt. Slogans like 'Under the paving stone lies a beach'; and *prenez-vous ca que vous desire pour la realite*. (Funnily enough, years later in France I saw in the Orange branch of the Credit Agricole exactly the same slogan used to advertise personal loans.) I saw the whole thing slowly take shape.

There was never a big overnight change. It wasn't a case of a lorry-load of new stuff—all rubber and zips and suspender belts—turning up one day. It appeared piecemeal because—

despite the takings of a Saturday – they just didn't have the finance to cover that kind of operation.

There was no party or anything for the reopening. One day it was just open again. And all the old crowd returned. They'd often come past the shop to see when it was going to open up again.

Fortunately, Vivienne had argued Malcolm out of one of his crazier ideas. He wanted to have an intercom by the front door and only let people in by appointment. This was mad. Someone pointed out that it would stop passers-by popping in to buy something. That got home to him. He certainly wasn't going to miss the chance of making a few bob out of someone with money to spend.

As a 16-year-old still at school I wasn't too sure about it all. I talked about it with my art teacher. He knew I worked with Malcolm because he was one of the few teachers I could have a conversation with about something more than homework or football.

How's the shop going? he asked one week.

Well, I said, they're getting into this rubber wear. He looked a bit concerned. Yeah, I said, I'm not too sure about it myself. Well, he said, you don't have to work there, you know. I agreed but then thought, yes I do, what else have I got going for me? Working there was my exit from the straight world.

Anyway, there was nothing really sordid about what we sold. It wasn't full of dildos like a Soho sex shop. Mind you, we did get some funny people coming into the shop. Because of all the rubber stuff, Malcolm had magazines like *Rubber Monthly* knocking around. Sometimes I'd have a flick through. They'd be full of stories about Wimbledon Common for some reason. We were there last weekend, they'd say, and the elements were against us, but we were snug from head to toe in our rubber suits.

The counter in the shop was a little kiosk with a till which stood slightly higher than the rest of the room. One day a bloke came in wearing a rubber mac, a real Wimbledon Common regular by the look of him. He stood there in front of the counter asking the price of things.

These rubber tights, he said. How much are they?

Ten pounds, I told him, noticing he had his hand in his pocket.

And these rubber suspenders?

Fifteen pounds.

His eyeballs popped. Fifteen *pounds*! he screeched and rushed out of the shop. He'd come his whack and there was this trail of spunk behind him all over the floor.

We always had trouble like that. It was horrible. You'd go into the changing rooms after someone had tried on some rubber tights and there'd be cum all over them. Vivienne would pick them up and say, it's alright. I'll just wash them down and put them back on the rack.

This was when Chris Spedding, the guitarist, started hanging out in the shop. Partly he'd be in because he was really into leather himself and partly he was there because his girl-friend of the time, Nora—who now lives with Johnny Rotten—was in the shop just about every day.

For ages Bernie maintained he already knew her from somewhere but couldn't quite place it. Eventually he remem-bered—he'd seen her hanging out with Jimi Hendrix in the six-ties. So Nora went from Jimi to Chris to Rotten.

She was German and a right pain. She'd come in, pick up a rubber skirt and say, haff you ziss in one leetle size bigger?

I'd say, it's the only one we've got and we're not getting any more.

So she'd try it on and it wouldn't fit. Two days later she'd be back, picking up the same rubber skirt and saying, haff you got ziss in one leetle size bigger?

She was always in the shop. I didn't twig at the time but really she just wanted to hang out in the shop and she was com-ing up with any old excuse she could find to be in there.

Spedding was just another person on the scene. I wasn't really aware of who he was, he was just a kind of mate. Steve and Paul were more in awe of him than me because of all his work with Roxy Music. But as far as I was concerned, he was just another rockabilly who'd park his flash motor out front and seemed to have more money than all the rest of us put together. Malcolm was his friend too.

Apart from Nora and the weirdos we'd get people buying it for their girlfriends, as a laugh. Some girls, those who were a bit more out there, would buy the rubber wear for themselves. Others would buy it for a fancy dress party or a dare.

Also there were the people who'd been coming into the shop when it was still Let It Rock. As well as the teds, there were always a few young art school types who were interested in the idea of teddy boy style.

They weren't so hidebound. They didn't say, as the teds did, I can only wear a drape. They'd mix it a bit, getting into biker stuff and cap-sleeved T-shirts. Others were into the glam rock idea and liked the idea of Sex.

It was about this time that Vivienne began to get really evangelistic about it all. Although the shop was a bit of an Aladdin's cave, something of a tot shop with all kinds of different clothes hanging around – some from Let It Rock, some from Sex – she really got into the idea of there being a party line. Sometimes she'd lay right into somebody.

I remember one bloke who was part of a working class West London crowd that had been coming into the shop since the early days. They'd started out as mods but gradually drifted into fifties Americana and then the Alan Ladd suits. A lot of them used to come in and religiously buy something every week.

They always had money because they left school early and went to work, mainly as builders and labourers. They played hard as well. They'd meet at The Roebuck, the same pub that everyone from the shop used, on Saturday lunchtime, then go down the Kings Road spending their money. Which could be quite a bit as they all still lived at home with their mums and dads. Some of them even made enough to run hot rod cars.

One of them came in, looked at the rubber gear and said,

cor, I don't know about this any more, this is all a bit too weird for me.

He'd changed his way of dressing as well. He'd been buying his clothes at Acme Attractions up the road a stall which generally did exactly the same as Malcolm only six months later, and were quite open about it. He had on what you'd now call a yuppie look – baggy trousers and braces.

When he started saying what he felt about the new clothes, Vivienne piled into him. Oh you, you look like you should be in a fucking potting shed, she said. Not in my shop. If you don't like it, get out.

Working for Malcolm and Vivienne was like being in the army. You felt as if you'd signed the Official Secrets Act. There were all these agitprop politics that you had to toe the line about. Fuck it, I often thought, it's only a fucking Saturday job.

Towards the end of my career in retailing, when we were gigging as a band, I was late quite a few times. Once I got in well hungover at four in the afternoon when I should have been there at 11. Well, Malcolm, I said, I can't do this any more, it's quite obvious. Vivienne got furious. What's up with you? she said, don't you want to work here? You realise it's a privilege to work here?

Of course I said yes because I needed the money. But their attitude that you had to be part of their camp used to get to me. It was just like the phrase that Thatcher was so fond of. 'One of us.' No bleeding difference between Thatcher and Westwood.

I never really got to know Vivienne. She was the most obtuse person I ever met. Once she told me about sending her kids to boarding school and asked me what I thought. Well, I said, sounds like Stalag 13 to me. Stalag what? Stalag 13. What do you mean? Stalag 13 was a prisoner of war camp. So? Well, the school with its rules sounds like a POW camp. (Plus I knew one of the kids was trying to escape all the time.) It can't be much fun being locked up there. It really sounds like a POW story. What do you mean? she said. At that point I gave up.

She was always in Malcolm's shadow. They say that gen-
tile women who marry Jewish men become more Jewish than
Jews. That's a good parallel for Vivienne and Malcolm. He was
a radical so she had to be even more radical.

Malcolm was impressive though. You'd find yourself copying him and his mannerisms. When he first started selling peg
trousers he developed a stance to show them off. He'd bend his
legs at the knee and stand half turned.

I found myself copying, as did everyone else who worked
in the shop. Not because we thought it was great but because
it was just so infectious.

And it was so stupid. I'd stand in the lunch queue at school
in my pegs while everyone else was in these horrible big flares.
I'd adopt the Malcolm stance. Far from looking cool I must
have looked like I'd done a packet in my trousers.

People often remark on how alike John and Malcolm look
these days. Well, I'm sure John did pick up on certain mannerisms that Malcolm had, not deliberately but because Malcolm
did that to people.

We were just in our early twenties by the time I left The
Pistols, beginning to find our way in the world, starting to get
more confidence. It's not that Malcolm was a father-figure to
us—as some have said—he was more like an elder brother
who'd actually been out there in the world and done it so he
had the confidence and experience. So we looked up to him like
that.

We'd hang out with him all the time. He liked being with
Steve and Paul because they were like his bit of rough. He was
a middle class radical who fancied the idea of being around two
real street kids.

We'd drink in The Roebuck, just up the Kings Road from
the shop, every Saturday straight after work. We'd sit around
chatting for a bit then go on to whatever was happening that
evening.

We'd go on to gigs or to parties or out to eat. One time we
went to The Last Resort in Fulham Road. Malcolm was pissed

and agreed to pay for everyone's meal. He was never tight-fisted but it wasn't often he was that generous.

So we all dived right in, me, Steve and Paul, and Wally. We ordered so much we couldn't eat the last dish they brought us, couldn't even touch it. Vivienne got really angry. You're just being greedy, you lot, she shouted, your eyes are bigger than your bellies. Fuck it, we thought, it's the first time Malcolm's splashed out and Vivienne's coming on at us like some kind of school ma'am, and Malcolm wasn't bothered, he was past caring.

On the other hand, Vivienne gave me an early insight into Malcolm's history. As I was applying to art school I needed a reference so I told Vivienne that I thought I'd ask Malcolm, since he was my employer. Oh no, she said, you don't want to ask Malcolm. He's been thrown out of every art school in London and some that aren't.

Around that time I came across a dog-eared treatise on the 1968 student uprisings, in particular the London School of Economics sit-in. One day I was browsing through it in the shop. Malcolm saw me and said, hey, what are you reading, boy? I showed him. He smiled. Oh, he said pretty casually, I'm in that.

He wouldn't say any more. I had to find out for myself. I read on paying great attention, trying to find out what he meant. The only passage I could find which could have referred to him was a section describing a debate during the LSE sit-in when the students were deciding whether to break down a pair of iron gates which lead to the bursar's office. The idea was they were after the records which the college held on all students.

They couldn't come to a decision so they put it to the vote when—as the book put it—a pair of bearded anarchists, one with flame red hair, appeared out of nowhere and took their decision for them, smashing down the gates with sledgehammers. Malcolm and his old friend Jamie Reid? Malcolm would neither confirm nor deny it.

From then on, I took more interest in him, looking at him

as more than just my employer. I began to understand him a little. The rubber clothing, for example, I never saw as part of his own sexual fantasy world, but as part of the fascination he had with all secret worlds.

He saw rubber fetishism as one of the few remaining genuine underground cultures. Simple as that. And he always wanted to be in on any underground culture going. He was like a kid making his camp under the dining room table with some blankets and pillows. Everybody would be sitting there round the table having their Sunday dinner while down below them the kid would think he had the only important world to himself. I always thought Malcolm was a bit like that kid.

For example, he wanted to be a member of as many clubs—of any description—as possible. Give him an unknown society, any society, and he wanted in. He'd take you to places like The Candy Box, just off Carnaby Street.

It opened at three o'clock in the morning, a club purely for hookers and people who worked in other clubs. They'd go there after work for a drink and a few rock stars would turn up. A real den of iniquity, it's divided up into several little catacombs. It's absolutely horrible but Malcolm would insist on taking you there because it made him feel part of some secret society.

Both Vivienne and Malcolm were also very good at using people. Malcolm was really into doing good window displays for the shop, often influenced by the ones Mr Green used to do for his Vince's Man's Shop in Soho—which was the first boutique ever, bringing faded blue denim and hipster trousers to the British public in the fifties.

Once we did a window together, just made a waste-paper basket out of chicken wire and hung shoes off it. I had a day off and when I came back there was a big trophy sitting there in the shop. Where did that come from? I asked. These people came in yesterday, he told me, who were judging a competition for the best window displays in the Kings Road. And I won. Not we won, you notice, but I won. Thank you, Malcolm.

They also really used me over the T-shirts which got them

busted and persuaded them to change the shop name from Sex to Seditionaries. There were different sorts of T-shirts, each with an image and a slogan or comment on the status quo, some of which Malcolm designed and some of which were designed by Bernie and Malcolm together.

There were the cowboy ones—two rough riders facing each other with their enormous dicks hanging out in front of them like door handles with a caption. There was the Cambridge Rapist in his mask with references to 'A Hard Day's Night'—the idea was to link it to the death of The Beatles' manager, Brian Epstein, during a supposed bout of homosexual S&M.

And there was a third T-shirt, which featured a black bloke clutching a basketball, with his 12-inch, semi-erect dick hanging down like a Nigerian salami. Muggins got the colour separations done for that at art school.

I felt a right prannet doing that. Vivienne—with Bernie backing her up as Malcolm was in the States, having extended his visit after striking up a rapport with The New York Dolls at the time—talked me into doing it. The trouble was, although they'd got me to do it—maybe because they knew it would save them money, or maybe because you can't get that kind of work done by your usual process shop—I didn't know how to do colour separations.

I knew what they were. A photographic process which breaks a picture down into four colours—well, three colours plus black— and lots of little dots. That's how all photographs are reproduced, be it for T-shirts or newspapers or books. That I knew.

But I had no idea how to make them, so I had to ask my tutor and show him the work. He took a look at this picture of a black bloke with this dick practically touching his knees and said, Glen, fancy an extra tutorial one day soon?

So I kept telling Vivienne and Bernie that I'd lost the keys to my locker. That way, I figured, I couldn't do the work. Bernie laid right into me, telling me I was stupid for losing them. Then Vivienne joined in and the three of us had a big slanging

match. Partly, I wasn't doing the work because I thought my
tutor had decided I was a poof but, more importantly, I was
dragging my feet because I wasn't keen on the work itself.

I told Vivienne I thought it was stupid, just childish. It
wasn't real outrage, it was cod outrage, like scribbling obscenities on the wall. There was something fascist about it. Quite
what, I don't know. I couldn't explain it very well at the time
and I still can't. But Vivienne came down on me like a dragon.
You, she said, you're a fascist.

I felt really used. I was the one who had to take it to my
tutor, not them. It was all down to them thinking, oh, Glen's
at art school, perhaps he can get it done for us. Not being paid
wasn't a problem; what was however was that I was being
used for the donkey work without any consultation on the artistic side of it. And that was important to me.

When they did make up the T-shirts—as I backed down
and did the separations—they got busted for sedition, which
was an obscure act of whenever. The actual person who got
them busted was Alan Jones—not the artist but a gay guy on
the scene, known as Leather And Bones Jones, a regular
enough guy.

He got busted and they got done as well. The thought of
the bust always struck me as hilarious. The idea of a regular
Mr Plod seeing Leather And Bones walking down the road in
his T-shirt and saying, here my lad, you're being seditious,
come with me.

Malcolm got really paranoid, deciding that there was a
conspiracy out to get him. He decided to shift all the T-shirts.
As I had a twelfth-hand Hillman Imp at the time I drove him
down to his place in South London. He'd just sold his jukebox
so we had the back seat piled up with records from it.

Just as we were crossing Chelsea Bridge we were stopped
by the police at a road block. Christ, I thought, just my luck:
no tax, bald tyre, I'm going to get done. Malcolm saw it differently. See, he said, I told you you shouldn't have come this
way.

He didn't care about me. But we both got out of it. When

the copper peered in the back and said, that's a lot of records, what are you going to do with them? Paul, who was in the back, piped up, plain as anything, play them. The copper said, oh yeah, right. Having been made to look stupid, he let us go without even checking up on the tax or the tyre. Or even getting to see the T-shirts.

Malcolm taught me things as well. Things like how not to mouth off about any ideas you might have. There's always people out there ready and willing to nick them.

People were always coming into the shop looking for things to copy. Don Letts – who then worked for Acme Attractions and was until recently part of Big Audio Dynamite – was always in. Which probably had something to do with the way that what we sold would reappear *slightly* redone in Acme six months later.

We'd always have to be slinging people out. They'd come in prowling around. At first you'd think they were just looking but really they were turning things over and over in their hands to see how they were made and checking out the cut so they could rip them off.

The worst one I remember was a woman whose company had a small place in the rag trade ghetto round the back of Oxford Circus. Malcolm had designed a very nice women's mac. A real fifties style, it was made of very thin ciré and looked almost like a dress, with its circular skirt and stand-up collar. It was like something that The B-52's might have worn half a dozen years later.

This women's firm had totally ripped it off for one of the mid-market youth fashion houses. And made a mint out of it. Without paying a penny to Malcolm and Vivienne whose idea it was. Well, sort of. They probably ripped it off themselves from a Hollywood still. But that's not the point really. Theirs was a fully-developed idea and garment.

Things like that made them really cagey, hence I was always having to lob people out of the shop if they looked like they were examining the clothes too closely. And I certainly learned the value of keeping my mouth shut about any ideas I might have.

That was probably another of the reasons why they became so obsessed with loyalty, with the idea that you were part of some élite squad. That obsession, if anything, became more intense over the years.

The bondage suits, for instance, were based on the idea of the strait-jacket, with trousers to match. Straps on the arms and legs could be fastened to restrict your movement. They came in right at the end of the period I spent working there. I never owned one myself – although I'd sometimes wear one in the shop. I thought they were stupid. How the fuck are you supposed to run for a bus in this was what I thought – a bit more down-to-earth than Malcolm and Vivienne.

Their attitude was, when you buy it you make a commitment to buying it and you wear it. Which was another part of Vivienne's 'One Of Us' schtick. If you weren't, fuck off.

But, even if you were, you had to buy the whole manifesto. It never seemed to enter their minds that someone might like to buy a pair of trousers from Sex and a shirt from somewhere else. You had to buy everything from them. They were quite totalitarian in their own way.

I thought the Sex stuff was a bit weird but not so weird that I didn't want to get involved with it. It *was* interesting.

I was along for the ride. I took from it what *I* liked – just as John later added safety pins to his jackets and T-shirts. Which was how most people treated the shop. They took from it what they felt they could handle – or wanted to handle, or could put to some use – and rejected the rest. As far as I was concerned, the bits I rejected I just didn't bother with.

5

Peeping Steve

It was around this time that Nick Kent started coming down to the rehearsals at Riverside. He was the star writer on the *NME* then and always in the shop because he was a Keith Richards clone and our shop was the last one in the Kings Road before Granny Takes A Trip, where all the Keith Richards clones bought their clothes.

Marty and Jean who ran Granny Takes A Trip were mates of Malcolm's and they all used to meet up after work in the pub. Sometimes Nick would be there too and we got talking to him.

Malcolm used to court him. As he was the *NME*'s star writer I guess Malcolm realised that once the band really started to get going, Nick would be able to help us out whether he knew it or not. Mind you, Malcolm did take the piss out of him as well, calling him Troy Tempest in a leatherjacket.

Probably because it was a way of roping him in for the future, Malcolm invited him down to a few rehearsals. We'd jam, going through things like 'I Can Feel The Fire' from Ron Wood's solo album which was out around that time. And we'd knock out things like 'Slow Death' by The Flamin' Groovies—who also used to come in the shop now and again when they were in town.

Then one day Malcolm said to me, what's going on with

this Nick bloke and the band? Not a lot really, he's come down and hacked through a couple of tunes with us. You sure that's all there is? He's been calling me up all hours of the day and night complaining about you guys, especially Steve. He reckons he's having to do all the work, write all the songs. He says you lot can't play and it's getting to him, it's too much work for him to take on, what with his writing and everything.

Sol had to go and put Nick straight, tell him that he wasn't even one of the band, just a mate who'd come and play with us every now and then.

I was still living with my parents at the time and I'd not long passed my driving test – with Bernie's assistance – so I borrowed my old man's Austin Cambridge one Sunday morning and drove over to Nick's. I got there at what I thought was a reasonable hour, around midday.

When I found the right place it was a real hole. A girl eventually answered the door. She looked exactly like Nick, only female. She had the same kind of eyes, a real pinned kind of look. I didn't realise what that was all about till long after.

She said, come in, but Nick's not awake yet, go up to his room. So I strode up there to have this man-to-man chat with Nick. I really like Nick, I thought, how am I going to explain this?

I started right in by saying there must have been a bit of a misunderstanding. He said, yeah, there has, which came as a great relief to me and we left it at that.

Fancy a drink then? he said.

A cup of coffee would be nice, I said.

He looked round the room and it was an absolute disaster area, stuff piled everywhere. But there was no kitchen and he sure as hell was in no state to get up, so I was wondering where he was going to get something to drink from.

Eventually he reached into his bedside table. Here it is, he said and pulled out a bottle of foul-looking medicine that could well have been the very stuff that Dr Jekyll used to turn himself into Mr Hyde. It probably wasn't bubbling and smoking away like a witch's cauldron but I certainly remember it that way. What was it? Kaoline and morphine or some such brew, apparently.

No thanks, Nick, I said. I think I'll be getting home for my dinner. Are we straight now then? Yeah, yeah. We both knew what the other one meant but we never said it in so many words. He didn't come down to rehearsals too much after that.

He was going out with Chrissie Hynde in those days. The first time I remember seeing her was in The Roebuck. Mike Smith, the singer and keyboard player in The Dave Clark Five, was having a quiet drink.

Chrissie knew who he was because she had a real background in screaming teeny bop stuff. I didn't realise then that The Dave Clark Five had been that enormous in the States.

Chrissie shouted to him, oi, where are your Beatle boots then? and started bashing out the rhythm to 'Glad All Over' on the table. Who's this? she said. He got so embarrassed he turned round and scuttled out. She didn't understand at all. Shit, she said, I would have liked someone doing that if I were him.

That summer I thought I was going to be able to work in the shop full-time up until I started at St Martin's School of Art in the autumn. But Malcolm suddenly gave the job to Chrissie instead. Because, I suppose, she was older and more rock 'n' roll with her leather jackets, whereas I was still at school and pretty straight.

But things started going a bit wrong before she could start. One day she was hanging around the shop when Nick Kent followed her in, angry. They'd had a row. He took his belt off and started whacking her with it. A bloke called Adrian happened to be in there as well. A supposedly famous photographer in the sixties, he was now most famous for the farce and frequency of his suicide attempts. Once he jumped from a roof and managed to land on the soft top of a passing van. It merely broke his fall and carted him a couple of miles up the road.

But this day he was all action, stepping right up to Nick and thumping him hard. Nick crawled away. Adrian spent the next hour nursing his fist and repeating over and over and over again, I hit him, I hit him, at last I've done something.

That was a quiet summer for the band. Steve had been nicked and was in prison – Ashford Remand Centre – for a while. He'd been thieving again, of course, but it was no big deal really.

Certainly not compared to the time he got caught messing around on the roof of Battersea Power Station trying to nick the lead. Someone saw him and called the police. When they arrived he shimmied right to the very top of one of the chimneys. A copper chased him up there. When he caught Steve he asked him what he thought he was up to. Well, said Steve, my mum and dad have split up. She's moved in with another man who's an ex-boxer who knocks me around. I've had enough of it and I wanted to be alone. The police considered this and took him down to the station – for tea and sticky buns.

Because there was so little going on with the band I arranged to give myself a bit of a holiday. A girl I was seeing pretty regularly had gone to France on an exchange visit to Tours. I took a job for a couple of weeks in a lino warehouse with the idea of getting some money together.

With the money I'd saved I went over to France, going straight to where she was staying in Tours. The idea was that I'd go for a fortnight but when I got there she gave me the bum's rush so I spent a couple of miserable days in France and then hared it back to England.

When I got to London Chrissie was no longer working in the shop. I think what happened was that Nick had been hanging around waiting to get hold of her. Malcolm didn't think Chrissie being larruped with Nick's belt in his shop was good for business. So I got the weekday job again. Good old Nick, I thought, now I've got my old job back on direct account of him.

The Alex Harvey Band came into the shop quite a few times that summer. Chris Glenn, the bass player, bought his gold lurex socks from us. Then, on one occasion, Malcolm happened to be around when they came in.

50

He took one look at them and said, what are those blokes doing here? Get 'em out. Malcolm was really having a brain-storm. I had to go over to them and say, I'm sorry but we're going to have to close for a bit. Perhaps you could come back tomorrow. Fortunately, they were alright about it and sloped off.

I was used to suddenly closing up the shop anyway. When Chelsea turned out on a Saturday afternoon, if we didn't lock the door, we had all the football fans in the shop trying to nick stuff and screaming obscenities. So it was no skin off my nose, it was no big deal to shut up shop in the middle of the day.

But this was different. Malcolm, I said, what was that all about? Those blokes, he said, they were weird. I reckon they're from the Inland Revenue.

Malcolm, they're not.

How do *you* know? he said, implying I was only the shop lad and what did I know?

I said, I know because they're The Sensational Alex Harvey Band.

The Sensational what band? he said.

The Sensational Alex Harvey Band. They're a group. They've been playing The Marquee every week. They're really good actually. You should come and see them.

Are you sure?

Yeah.

Well, what do they want? A pair of creepers, maybe. Or some socks. Or a T-shirt. Alright then, he said, but watch 'em.

A couple of months later he did come to the Hammersmith Odeon with Bernie and me to see them play. I could see the re-lief on his face when he realised they really were a band.

That autumn, I started my foundation course at St Martins, which is in Charing Cross Road, right opposite all the mu-sical equipment shops in Denmark Street, London's Tin Pan Alley. Because of that it was inevitable that sooner or later I would be delegated by Steve and Paul to fence some of the gear they'd purloined. And they did delegate me, of course, handing me a guitar to get rid of.

I took it to a couple of shops who just weren't interested and then to Macaris who seemed to be interested in buying it but who were being a bit funny about it to me.

The bloke behind the counter said, look, I've just got to go and look up the year of manufacture, I'll be back in a couple of minutes, I've got to check the price. He'd come back and make another excuse to keep me hanging around.

Then the young assistant started giving me funny looks, as if there was something up and I should know there was something up. He couldn't actually tell me what was going on because that would put him in shtuck but he was trying to tip me the wink.

I realised I was going to be nicked. I've never been nicked before, I thought, I wonder what it's like? So I hung around and, sure enough, a few minutes later a squad car turned up, all its lights flashing.

They handcuffed me. You don't need to bother with them, I said, I won't run off. Oh, yes you will, they said. Not stupid, coppers, are they?

But this time they were wrong. I was really curious to know what it was like to have your collar felt. I guess I was trying to earn a couple of lowlife brownie points, so I could catch up with Steve and Paul's criminal pedigree.

As it was right across the road from college everyone was hanging out the window to see what was happening. All my mates, my tutor, everyone saw me bundled into the back of the squad car.

They took me to West End Central and, instead of telling them what had really happened, I gave them a story. I said I'd bought it off a bloke in The Roebuck. They swallowed it and said they were charging me with handling stolen goods.

Just like in cop shows there was a nice cop and a nasty cop. The nice one – who was a dead ringer for the compère in *Hi-De-Hi* – came in and said, Well Glen, we've thought about it, we're not going to charge you with handling stolen goods. Great, I thought. No, we're going to charge you with theft. If I plead guilty to that, I thought, I'll end up in the nick for the rest of my life. But he told me that, in the eyes of the law, theft is actually a lesser charge than handling stolen goods. If there weren't people handling stolen goods then nobody would nick things in the first place. At least that's how they figured it and that's how he explained it to me.

I went up before the beak at Great Marlborough Street magistrates court. Again they swallowed my story and gave me a year's conditional discharge. Oh, I piped up, does that mean I get off? No it does not, young man, snapped the magistrate in no uncertain terms and explained how it all worked to me.

As I was leaving I made a big show of asking to see the guitar one more time. I paid good money for that, I said, can't I just have a last go on it? They let me have one last look and told me that it belonged to someone in another band – which made me feel really guilty.

Then they said, you're at art college, you must be able to draw. You could do a drawing of the gentleman in question you claim you bought the guitar from. Maybe they meant it, maybe they were teasing. They said that it was in everyone's interest that he got caught.

So I just made up a face, drew it for them. Now luck would have it that my drawing was spot on for a guy who drank in The Roebuck. Plus it turned out that he was a speed dealer.

The kids in the band whose guitar it really was set up a look-out in The Roebuck and, of course, they spotted him. The dealer got more and more paranoid sitting there, noticing these two guys in the corner who kept looking at a bit of paper then at him, then having a bit of a conflab.

He got so paranoid he decided to leg it. The kids immediately followed him thinking this was proof that he was the right guy. Act guiltily and they'll judge you guilty. As they started to follow him down the street he got more and more worried. He broke into a run. So they took off after him, caught him and gave him a hiding. But, of course, it was entirely the wrong bloke. They should have been chasing Steve Jones.

Slowly we began to take the whole idea of the band more seriously. We'd try and come up with ideas of what it was all about – sometimes prompted by Bernie, sometimes not. For example, we decided to pay attention to the way we looked so we all had our hair cut short – except Wally – and took to wearing Hush Puppies and jeans, a kind of mod look – which was odd considering that Malcolm had a shop which specialised in teddy boy gear. But what it shows is how, right from the earliest days, we were always much more than assembly line workers in Malcolm McLaren's dream factory.

Our next major step was to sort out a name. Before I'd joined they'd called themselves Strand – after the Roxy Music song 'Do The Strand' – and The Swankers, but both these names were well past their sell-by date by the time I arrived.

Yet, although we hadn't thought of a name, we'd started to fancy doing a couple of gigs and, of course, you can't do gigs without a name. Our idea was that we should call ourselves The All Stars. As it would only be a temporary name we felt it didn't really matter all that much what we called ourselves.

Malcolm was about to go to the States. This was to be the visit on which he linked up with The New York Dolls. Eventually he took over their management and put them into red patent leather suits, effectively driving the last nail into The Dolls' coffin.

So it was Bernie we got talking to in the pub about a name for the band. He was adamant. No, no, no, no, no, he said, it's got to be the real thing, you've got to start out as you mean to go on. Get it right from the beginning. Get the correct name and stick with it. Everything flows from there.

So that put the damper on gigs for a bit.

Some time before, Malcolm had come up with a list of half a dozen names. The Damned was one. Kid Gladlove was another. A third was Crème De La Crème. Blimey leave it out Malcolm, said Steve when he heard that one, that sounds more like some poncey wine bar.

And there was QT Jones And The Sex Pistols. As well as

the pun, I'm sure the reason Malcolm chose QT was that it was the postal code around where Steve – who was still the singer at this point – was staying.

The rest of the name was quite straightforward. Pistols was a strong, hard word, not bad for a band's name. Sex, of course, came from Malcolm's shop. He was never shy of a bit of cross-promotion.

I'm also sure another influence was Disco Tex And His Sex-O-Lettes. They had a big hit around the time and the shop was always full of these kids who were really into that gay, shallow disco – stuff like 'The Hustle'. These kids would hang out in The Sombrero in Kensington High Street and Chaguer-amas in Covent Garden – which became The Roxy Club a couple of years later.

So we didn't think much of it as a name at first but while Malcolm was away in the States, we somehow came round to it and decided to go with it. Sex Pistols it was. We dropped the QT Jones bit and, by the time Malcolm came back, we were really quite up about it.

A lot happened around that time. We got a name, we left Riverside and we slung Wally out of the band. The three things which really set us up for John's arrival.

I got on quite well with Steve around that time. You hungry? he said one day. Come on then, I'll treat you. He took me to a pie and mash shop on Hammersmith Broadway. I was starving so I had pie and mash twice. He had *double* pie and *double* mash twice.

As we waddled, full as pillows, back to Riverside, I said, I thought you were skint. Well, he said, I found this attaché case, see. Yeah? And it had a grand in it.

Steve was also a major factor in our leaving Riverside. What happened was, when we'd go there to rehearse on a Friday night, he would disappear for an hour or so.

One week we decided to follow him to find out where he was sloping off to. We found him on the roof ledge peering down at people in a car below. As this was something of a lovers' lane, he had a good chance of catching a couple knobbing on the back seat. And Steve, as I'd already found out for myself, always did like a bit of voyeurism.

Unfortunately, soon after that a copper spotted him doing his Peeping Tom bit, followed him inside the studios and looked very strangely at all this expensive gear lying around.

So we would have had to leave anyway, in case the cops started taking too close an interest in it. But we also had to leave because we chucked Wally out of the band. As the place was really his we couldn't use it without him. We'd been talking about it for ages and Bernie was always badgering us about it – but we'd not really done anything about it.

The crunch came when Malcolm returned from America. He put his foot down straightaway. I told you to sack Wally before I left, he said. How come he's still in the band? I won't have anything more to do with you lot till you give him the elbow. Which we did.

I never really minded Wally. When push came to shove, I stuck up for him. Then Paul said, I don't know why you're sticking up for him, he's been trying to get you slung out on your ear for ages. So that was it, really. Wally left the band.

He's a strange bloke though. He still calls me up now and again. Not long ago he was on the phone to me moaning about Paul saying, he won't give me the time of day. Which, given the way Wally rambles on, is scarcely surprising.

Then he started on me. I made them what they are today, he said. Without me The Pistols would have been nowhere. I'm going to take them to court and sue them.

What's all that about then, Wally?

The group was all my idea. Before they met me, Steve and Paul were just petty criminals, didn't know nothing about nothing. I told 'em what to do, I told 'em.

What did you tell them, Wally?

They used to nick things like shoes, bits of jewellery and cars. Now, what's the good of nicking a car if you can't drive it and you've got to ditch it? So I told 'em. Guitars. That's what they should be nicking. If it hadn't been for me they'd never have nicked any guitars and there would have been no group.

56

So you're going to stand up in front of a judge and say all that, are you, Wally?

No, not exactly.

With Wally out of the band we could really take it seriously. But for a while we found it hard. Without him we had to struggle along with just the three of us. Steve was doing OK but he was finding it hard to play guitar at the same time as singing. Not that he was playing any flash lead parts but to keep a strong rhythm part going and sing at the same time is rather like having to twiddle both your thumbs in opposite directions at the same time. So we decided we had to look for a new singer.

6

I'll Kill You

'll kill you, said John on the phone in his best whine. It was his first rehearsal with the band and none of us had turned up. We'd booked The Crunchy Frog, which was a hippy commune/warehouse/community centre by the Thames in Rotherhithe down in South East London, but we couldn't be bothered to go.

We'd been using it for a while since we had to leave Riverside Studios, trying out a couple of new singers. But all to no avail.

It was a bloody long way to go across London. The last time I'd been there I nearly got caught bunking my fare. Every time I changed trains there was a posse of London Underground inspectors, so I had to keep doubling back on myself. It took me about three hours to get six stops.

So I decided to give it a miss that day. I really didn't fancy schlepping all the way down there. Steve and Paul didn't bother either. Only John and his mate, John Grey, turned up. John never went anywhere by himself, there was always an entourage.

I was deputed to phone him up and apologise. That's when he threatened to kill me. But I cooled him out and he agreed to come along to a new rehearsal place that we'd found, The Rose And Crown in Wandsworth.

That's where we really started rehearsing together properly as the band. Where we got the money to pay for it, I'm not quite sure. Perhaps Malcolm coughed up. He was certainly very keen that we have John in the band. Or maybe we sold some of the gear.

There weren't that many rehearsal places around at that time which we could afford. But this one was cheap so we booked a full week. Our idea was that at last we could have a real go at it, make sure things worked out.

But they didn't work out. The landlord had obviously decided he could make a lot of money out of this rehearsal room lark. So he'd taken an upstairs room and divided it into six spaces, figuring he could charge £1.50 an hour for each of them and really coin it in.

What he didn't understand was the nature of rock music. It's loud. And he hadn't put any sound-proofing in. There were just hardboard partitions between the rehearsal rooms—cubicles really. Nothing substantial enough to stop the noise going straight downstairs into the bar.

Every time we struck a chord people would come tearing up from the bar to tell us to turn that fucking racket down. And we'd say, we're paying good money for this. Nothing really constructive got done there. But it was where we first had a serious go at turning ourselves into a real band.

We weren't doing nine to five but we were working every afternoon for a week. This new zeal was strange in a way because John wasn't really our idea, but Malcolm's.

John had turned up one day in the shop. Malcolm, who had been told to look out for him by Steve, was impressed. He arranged for us all to have a drink with him at The Roebuck. We trooped along and he more than likely brought his mate John Grey along with him.

He looked much the same as he did later, with a T-shirt and his 5000-volt haircut. We had a few drinks and all thought

60

he seemed a bit of a laugh so we asked him to come back to the shop with us and have a bit of a sing.

He was obviously nervous about it, but he came. We put a few records on the jukebox and got him to mime along. One of them, I remember, was Alice Cooper's 'Eighteen'. He stood there, shouting along and flapping his arms round like an over-excited seagull. He looked *just* like he did when we played real gigs. He was John Rotten from that very first moment.

But we still couldn't tell whether he could sing or not. It was a funny situation. He felt awkward and so he mostly just took the piss out of it to get through.

But we decided to try him out. This guy is the one, Malcolm said, and we went along with him. Who knows why? It certainly took us a while to understand John's plus points. When we first started with him, even when we were rehearsing properly with him, all we could think of was that he couldn't sing. Malcolm's got us this singer, we kept saying to each other, and he can't sing, what is all this about?

What we didn't realise at the time was that one of the main reasons that Malcolm was so keen on John was that he was so like Richard Hell – who was one of Malcolm's mates in New York. He was as near as dammit to being a stylistic carbon copy of Hell.

We knew Malcolm had been really impressed with Hell in New York because they kept up a correspondence. And, at one point, Malcolm must have asked him if he'd consider coming over to join the band, because Hell wrote to us via him saying that it sounded interesting but that because money and visas would be a problem he just couldn't.

But, at that time, none of us had seen Hell in person. We'd seen a picture of The Heartbreakers that Malcolm had brought back from New York – the one in which it was meant to look like they'd been shot in the heart but in fact looked like they'd all had the same accident with a ketchup bottle. But we hadn't seen him perform. And when we did, we all thought: aha, John, now we see.

Another person we thought of using as a front man was

Midge Ure – who I went on to work with straight after The Pistols, in The Rich Kids. Malcolm also made that contact when he and Bernie went on a trip up north, searching round textile factories for old fifties cloth to use for making up zoot suits. We had some extremely hot gear lying around so we asked them if they'd have a go at getting rid of it for us out of town where it maybe would have cooled down somewhat.

They ended up trying to sell a Marshall amp in Glasgow. The shop they went into wouldn't have anything to do with it though. They must have thought something was fishy. They certainly must have thought Malcolm was fishy, dressed as he was in black leather from head to toe. No one at that time in Glasgow had ever seen anything like it outside a porn mag.

Midge happened to be standing next to them in the shop where they got the bum's rush. Canny Scot that he is, he guessed what was happening, followed them out of the shop and offered them a tenner for the amp. Malcolm took note of the way he looked – with his hair all slicked back, a really avant-garde gesture in Glasgow when everyone else was in loon pants.

He told me about Midge when he got back to London and I called him from the shop one Saturday, telling him we'd be interested in him as a singer. But he wasn't interested in us. I would, he said, but I've got this thing called Slik just going.

So what made us persist with John? It's difficult to say. Maybe that very quickly he started coming up with lyrics and that he and I got on well right from the off. Well, not quite from the off. To begin with, he thought I was as close to Steve and Paul as they were to each other – and they were like a single amoeba that won't let anyone else into its world.

But, once he realised that I was a bit apart from them, we started to get on well and wrote a lot together, coming up with new lyrics for 'Did You No Wrong' and beginning to find cover versions that would really establish our identity.

From Steve and Paul's point of view, I reckon they thought he was a real card and that it would be a big laugh having him around.

62

The Sex Pistols' first photo session, Carnaby Street, London.
(Rex Features)

At the Sex shop: Steve Jones on the far left, Alan (Leather and Bones) Jones in the center with Chrissie Hynde to his right, Vivienne Westwood on the far right. (Rex Features)

The first recording sessions, at Majestic Studios, Clapham, in the early summer of 1976. Chris Spedding has yet to arrive. The band plus Malcolm and Nils Stevenson pose outside, like soldiers about to go over the top for the first time. (Rex Features)

A band meeting upstairs at the Sex Pistols' HQ in Denmark Street, London's Tin Pan Alley, around the time of the 'Anarchy' tour. John loafs on Glen's bed. (Bob Gruen)

Later the same day, downstairs at Denmark Street for a photo call—which is why Glen has only two strings on his bass. (Bob Gruen)

Even later the same day. John Rotten when he really did prefer tea to sex. (Bob Gruen)

Paul, wearing Glen's grey peg trousers. The message on the t-shirt is a Bernard Rhodes contribution to punk theory—'You're going to wake up one morning and decide what side of the bed you're on'. (Bob Gruen)

Steve at London's Lansdowne Studios during the 'Anarchy' sessions. The patched denim loon leg belongs to Kim Thraves, assistant to producer Dave Goodman. (Bob Gruen/Rex Features)

Malcolm modelling the first Sex Pistols promo t-shirt featuring
a young nude boy—in the Denmark Street courtyard.
(Bob Gruen/unknown)

Outside Denmark street, the band do their best Alvin Stardust impressions. (Bob Gruen)

Certainly John's arrival changed our attitude. Before he came along we'd mess around with songs like 'Build Me Up Buttercup', with me fiddling around on a little clavinet that we'd found knocking around somewhere, and Steve singing. With John in the band we began to search out songs which were really us.

Quite soon we had enough songs for a set. Some of which were cover versions that one or another of us had found. Some of which were songs John and I had written together.

But we still always had a problem finding somewhere to rehearse. We tried out The Roundhouse for a while, even interrupting a World Service broadcast which was going out live from somewhere else in the building while we were bashing through a rehearsal–probably our first public airing. So that didn't last long.

We tried lots of rehearsal spaces but they were all a rip off and totally out of the way. One day, flicking through the music papers like we did every Wednesday, I spotted an ad in the *Melody Maker* for premises in Tin Pan Alley–Denmark Street. I showed it to Malcolm and he said to call up and offer £1000 blind.

So I called. Here, I said, I think my mate's mad but he says to offer you £1000 for your place without ever seeing it. And the bloke on the other end of the phone said, I think we could talk business. Malcolm got right on the phone with him and sorted it out.

The bloke's name was Bill Collins, the father of Lewis Collins, star of *The Professionals* TV show. Bill had been a Beatles roadie and then became a manager, of The Mojos and Badfinger–which is how he came to be the owner of studios in Denmark Street.

Badfinger had worked out of the studios but the main guy topped himself in 1975 (to be followed by another in 1983) and Bill was left with a studio and no band.

His big thing though was his piano theory. He'd been involved with bands all those years and could play a bit of music but he never quite got the hang of the idea of written music.

So whenever he tried to explain any musical idea he just couldn't make his bands understand.

The classic example of that happened with Badfinger. They wrote a song called 'Without You', which they recorded as a semi-rock song. Bill's idea was that they should play it as a ballad instead. So he tried to show them on the piano. But as he couldn't play it that well, he just couldn't get his ideas across.

Which was a dreadful shame. They badly needed a hit at the time. (And it was that lack of hits which probably helped bring about the suicides.) They might have had one if Bill could have explained his idea because that's exactly what Harry Nilsson later did with the song, turned it into a big ballad and scored a number one hit with it.

So, frustrated by this inability to demonstrate his ideas, he developed an entire new musical theory. It had no sharps or flats and was based on a six-line stave instead of the five-line one which is usual for musical notation.

He then built a machine for the piano which had a series of lights which went on and off ensuring that you played the right note – without ever having to understand what a sharp or a flat was. He tried to get it marketed or patented but he never succeeded.

Anyway Malcolm quickly agreed to the terms on the lease and Steve and I moved in, living there as well as using it as a rehearsal room.

It was a small outbuilding off Denmark Street, behind a Greek bookshop. It looked like it had been built as a rag trade sweatshop at the turn of the century and was sandwiched between a musical equipment shop and The Tin Pan Alley Club – which was a notorious music biz drinking den. Amongst other things, we were always finding used syringes that had been lobbed over the wall. At the far end was St Giles Church – which meant we never had an excuse for being late anywhere as the bells tolled the hour – and the quarters – right through the night.

Inside there were two rooms, one on each floor, both the

same size, about 20 feet by 15. It was small and poky, the carpet stank of sweat from all the bands that had rehearsed there over the years, the floor was rotten and covered with fungus. More unpleasant smells came from the toilet that didn't work and the leaking skylight which let in so much rain the whole place was always damp. The windows had been bricked up as part of the soundproofing.

Squalid is the word. Steve and I shared the one room upstairs and tried to do it up a bit. We put in a new sink and Malcolm bought us a Baby Belling cooker, one electric ring on which we could heat a can of beans very, very slowly.

We fixed it up as well as we could, which wasn't well but it did give us both somewhere to live away from our parents, a first real taste of independence. And it meant we had a regular rehearsal space – which we used nearly every day. Maybe we'd only do half an hour before sloping off but, bit by bit, we were able to put a set together.

Our first gig was all of one hundred yards down the road. On November 6, 1975, we played support at St Martin's School of Art to a band called Bazooka Joe – which included a young man called Stuart Goddard, later to become Adam Ant and so obsessed by punk that he has an almost complete set of Seditionaries clothing.

We'd been moaning to Malcolm about wanting to play some gigs. Alright then, he said, if you're so keen, why don't you go and find them yourselves? I took him at his word.

At that point I'd just left St Martin's. I'd finished my foundation year earlier that summer and, although I'd been offered a full-time place – and grant – to do my Fine Art degree in painting, I blew it out.

I was proud of getting accepted, particularly at St Martin's because it was such a good art school, but Fine Art seemed a fast road to nowhere. What kind of job can you get at the end of that?

Even if you become a great painter you end up being some rich man's lackey, sponsored and dabbled with – if you're lucky. More likely you rot as a tutor in High Wycombe or somewhere like Hatherley School of Fine Art, teaching the talentless children of the rich.

When the band became serious, I thought this is a far more contemporary and interesting way to make an artistic statement. So I packed in art school.

Which was stupid really. And Vivienne kept telling me, I should have stayed on just for the grant. Which is what Mick Jones of The Clash did. He was at Hammersmith Art College. He turned up the first day of the term, picked up his grant, bought a guitar with it and then disappeared till the start of the next term and that term's grant cheque.

But it was because I'd been at St Martin's that we got that first gig. At the end of my foundation year I'd been voted in as Social Secretary, in charge of putting on all the shows there. So I trooped down there and muscled us in on the Bazooka Joe gig.

Then, just before that gig, I went over to Central School of Art in Holborn and swung us another gig there. I walked in through the door and, feeling a bit lost, I asked the first person I saw if he knew whether the Social Secretary was around.

Yeth, he said, I am. This was Sebastian Conran, son of Terence Conran, who founded Habitat, and brother of designer Jasper Conran.

But the bloke next to him wasn't having any of that. Yes, he said, *we* are, making it clear that they were joint social secretaries. This was Al McDowell who became a close friend of mine, founded *i-D* magazine and coined the phrase 'Fuck Art: Let's Dance.'

Why do you want the social sec? he asked.

I'm in a band and we're looking for a gig.

What's the name of the group? asked Al.

The Sex Pistols.

Sebastian's eyes lit right up. Oh yeth, he said, with a name like the Thex Pithtolth we mutht have you.

So I invited them to the gig at St Martin's. Which was something of a racket, plus Bazooka Joe kept on pulling the plugs on us trying to get us off the stage. And they were in the audience.

Al was dressed up like Bud Flanagan for some reason, almost drowning in a raccoon coat. And he kept roaring with laughter all the way through the set – well, what we managed to do of it. I really thought we'd blown it when I saw him cracking up. But, in fact, he really liked us.

The Central gig was the first one where we were actually allowed to play our own set all the way through. This time we were promoted to co-headliners, with Roogalator, who were another of the big names on the pub rock circuit at the time.

As soon as we arrived, the bass player, Paul 'Bassman' Riley, took one look at us and came over with a proposition. Instead of moving all the gear around, he said, how about if I borrow your bass cabinet?

OK, I said.

Er, he said, while we're about it, you couldn't lend me your bass as well, could you?

They were meant to be a pro group while we were just starting out. Yet we were the ones with all the flash gear. Which just shows you what a lot of stuff Steve had lifted for us.

The show itself was one of the best we ever played. On the other hand, though, I was really drunk so maybe I only remember it that way. John turned round to me at the end and said, I can't understand you. All the people I know, when they get pissed, they start fights, whereas you just seem really happy.

There you go, I thought, a solid illustration of the difference between John and myself.

All this time we were still trying to fix up Denmark Street so that it became vaguely comfortable. We got so fed up with the leaking roof that we decided to try and mend it with some tar. Steve had gone off somewhere so, to help me along, I nicked one of his black bombers, the capsules of speed he always had around.

He had a prescription for them, from an infamous doctor in Harley Street. They were meant to be for his weight but I'm not sure I believe that. I thought maybe he'd convinced Malcolm that he was overweight – which he wasn't – and Malcolm had this real thing about us looking the part. So Malcolm sprang for the script. And Steve got the free speed he was after.

Out of my box on this bomber, I remembered there was a bird I fancied at St Martin's – Virginia. So I went there and cornered her in the canteen and tried to chat her up for half an hour. I was rabbiting and rabbiting and rabbiting as we drank our tea. She quite obviously wasn't listening to a word of it.

Glen, she said, you alright, Glen? It was a freezing cold day and I'd been sitting there in nothing but these dungarees that I'd been working on the roof in. Never got anywhere with her, of course.

Steve was already there when I got back. He looked at me really carefully and deliberately. He got out his pills, tipped them out on the table and started counting them – which took absolutely ages because he never did count too well. Just as he got to the last one I said, by the way, I had one of those. That's how it is between flat mates.

Because someone had tried – very badly – to soundproof the room, all the walls were covered with cork tiles which stood proud from the wall behind. We took it all down in one day, helped by Steve's mothers' little helpers. All that was left to do was a big hole in the wall by the sink that needed filling.

We decided to go to bed for the night. We both got our heads down and then a scratching noise started up. Steve is that you? No, Glen is that you?

We turned the light on. The room was full of funny little animals whizzing all over the floor. Mice. A squadron of them moving four abreast in perfect formation, frightened because we'd put the light on, scampering around trying to jump over the bed and the settee. They'd been happy behind their cork and we'd torn down their cover. Whoooah, said Steve and dived under the covers.

We had to sleep like that. I had to try and get a bit of kip on the crumbling sofa with a torch in one hand and a big bit of four by two in the other, ready to whack any of the mice if they came out to get us. It was bad enough already sleeping there. In fact, it was fucking horrible. The roof leaked. Every time it rained you had to move your bed. And after that, of course, we couldn't get to sleep. Every little noise we thought was another assault wave of killer mice.

'Ere Glen, said Steve, you asleep?

No, can't.

Me neither. Glen, you ever had a wank with a johnny on?

Can't say I have, Steve.

It's fucking great. Mind you, better than that is a loaf of bread. Not sliced stuff though, none of that Wonderloaf lark. It's got to be a good loaf of bread, like that one you buy down the road, the black one, that'll do.

Slice the top off and scoop a bit out from the middle. Then fill it up with water from the kettle. Not boiling, mind, that could prove disastrous. Just a nice kind of warm, room temperature slosh of water, that's what you need. And you shag that. It's fucking great. The best thing of all though is . . .

Yeah?

Pound of liver with a slit in it.

Goodnight, Steve.

We were so broke when we were living there that I'd buy a bar of Kit Kat in the morning, have two fingers of it for breakfast and the other two for dinner in the evening. That's all I'd have to eat all day.

By this time I'd left St Martins so there was no more grant. I was having to survive on my dole money – which seemed to disappear the day I got it. Kit Kats were about all I could afford.

Then we sussed out that bread and milk were delivered to the local restaurants really early. So we'd wait up all night, follow the delivery van around and survive on the bread and milk we could swipe.

We complained to Malcolm, told him we were fed up with the mice and we didn't have enough money to eat properly.

(John, by the way, would always claim they were rats – with his usual sense of accuracy.)

So Malcolm went down Club Row market and bought us a cat and the most ridiculously horrible food – tins of sardines and those disgusting tinned plum tomatoes they used to try and make you eat at school. There you go boys, he said, that'll do you.

And he cooked us sardine soup. It wasn't bad, actually. Cor, he said, this is almost like being an art student again. But, that one banquet apart, it wasn't. We were always hungry.

One Sunday I was so fed up with living on Kit Kats that I called my mum. How you going, Glen? she said. Bit fed up actually, I'm hungry. Come over son, there's a nice bit of Sunday dinner going here.

Naah, I said, I can't make it, I've got to go and see a mate. But that was an excuse. Really my mouth was watering. The truth was I really fancied going there but I didn't even have the money to bunk the tube. All I needed was 10 pence – which was what you had to pay in those days if you said you came from the previous stop – but I didn't even have that. We were always hungry and we were always broke.

It's not as though we weren't making money at the time either. We were gigging and getting well paid for it. When we did start playing proper gigs we got surprisingly good money. We'd get £50 or £60 a night – which might not sound like a lot but that's still what young bands get for the same gigs today. In fact, a lot of bands starting out these days have to *pay* to play their first gigs. Which is a right liberty.

But we never saw any of that money. It got to the stage where we didn't bother to ask what happened to it. We didn't even think about it. Only once did I get some money after a gig. We'd played in St Albans and I'd met a girl there, Claire. She was the Social Secretary at the college who'd booked us in to play.

Give us a quid, Malcolm, I said, so I can get home in the morning. He gave me a fiver. I couldn't believe my luck. We went down to an awful Wimpy Bar opposite Chagueramas –

which later became The Roxy. In those days it was full of horrible camp types dancing to limp disco. They were all sub-'Virginia Plain' characters with half a floorbrush on each shoulder. It was supposed to look like they were wearing epaulettes but it never did.

That was the first time I'd had any money out of gigging in a year.

We played some strange old gigs in that period. Andrew Logan's party, for instance, which got us our first press – a mention in an upmarket society fashion magazine.

The party was held at his flat, which was a loft in a warehouse down by the river in Shad Thames on a wharf right next to Tower Bridge. I'd never seen anywhere like it. We had to take all the gear up in a hoist.

Then, when you got inside, you could see how this man had come to run something as bizarre as The Alternative Miss World – with its transvestites and concept artists. Logan had done some of the designs for the old Biba department store in Kensington High Street and, when it closed down, he took all his work back to his flat.

His bedroom was the Sleeping Beauty scene he'd done for Biba's children's department and the kitchen area was full of artificial trees – which his party guests used to piss against.

I thought it was great. Unsurprisingly, Steve looked around and said: bum bandits, all of 'em. Come on, said Malcolm, be cool, he's letting us play here. But Steve really wasn't happy. This wasn't his idea of a proper place for his band to play. When we did get to play, the stage was a set that Logan had designed for a movie – the court scene in Derek Jarman's *Sebastiane*.

We played The Marquee for the first and only time supporting Eddie And The Hot Rods. We were dreadful – but arrogant with it. It was the first time we'd had proper monitors on stage – which meant it was the first time John heard his own voice. And he didn't like what he heard. So he trashed the monitors.

A terrible gig. But also our first review. Neil Spencer wrote about it in the *New Musical Express* beneath the headline 'Don't Look Over Your Shoulder, But The Sex Pistols Are Coming.'

You can't play, a French tourist at the front shouted.

So what? I shouted back.

Later Spencer chatted to us, asking about music. We're not into music, we told him.

What are you into then?

Chaos.

We quickly found that few places would let us play so we started looking round for alternatives. Malcolm had taken on an assistant by this time, Nils Stevenson. He wanted to give Nils something to do to justify his position so he sent him out to hunt out unusual places for us to play.

Nils came up with El Paradise, a strip club in Soho's Brewer Street. It fitted. The Sex Pistols plus strip club. What could be more natural?

We took it over for a Sunday night, hiring it, promoting the gig ourselves, pushing out a lot of handbills. And, on the day itself, we turned up early to sort out the club.

It was a tiny place – nothing more than a shop knocked through from the street at ground level, no more than 60 feet long. At one end was a small bar from which we sold orange juices on top of the counter with the booze tucked away underneath.

At the other end was a stage with footlights. To one side was a row of lights which flickered on and off like something you'd get at the Palladium – a cheap trick to try and convince the punters that they were in somewhere far classier than was really the case.

And it stank. It was absolutely filthy, horrible and scuzzy, with disgusting stains on the floor. So – hard as it may be for some people to believe – we disinfected the whole place, sloshing the stuff everywhere.

When it came to show time, John started acting very oddly. Either because he had the hump or because he thought it would make for a good show he started smashing the foot-lights one by one.

As he did this a Maltese feller started striding slowly but purposefully towards us from the back of the club. We knew he was the owner of the club and – while he can't have been more than four-foot-nine inches tall – we knew that Soho was run by Maltese gangsters just like him.

He was built like a brick shithouse and he plonked himself down right in front of the stage. He put one elbow on the stage itself and stared straight at John. There was a fair crowd there but it was scarcely crowded: John couldn't have not noticed him.

But that's what he pretended. For three numbers the Maltese heavy stared at him – while all his henchmen stood at the back of the club watching him watching John. For three numbers John looked everywhere but at him. Finally, his point made – a kind of behave yourself young lad, or you will come to a sticky end – he stood up and wandered back to the bar.

It was also during this period that we had the strangest set of photographs taken of us, by Peter Christopherson who worked for a design company, Hipgnosis – whose offices were at the back of our Denmark Street HQ – and who later joined Throbbing Gristle, a band best known for tabloid spreads on their occult practices.

Their offices faced right onto our living quarters and they were always staring at us. It got so bad we had to do the full old lady bit and put up net curtains.

Then one day the main guy who'd been peeking at us turned up and asked if he could take some pictures of us. Malcolm said OK, but even he can't have had any idea what Christopherson intended.

Paul, he made up covered with bullet wounds. Steve, he photographed in handcuffs. John, he put in a straitjacket. And me, he took me round to the YMCA locker room and photographed me half dressed. It was pretty obvious he was after making me look like a rent boy. A very weird man – who, if The

Pistols had stayed together, could have made a fortune flogging those snaps to a Sunday dreadful.

Apart from our regular rehearsals we often found ourselves at a loose end and would all troop round together. One afternoon we were all wandering up Tottenham Court Road for some reason. Maybe we were on our way to a cheap Indian self-service restaurant that Malcolm had introduced us to. Maybe we were on our way to the Fender Soundhouse because Steve needed some new strings for his guitar.

About half way up Tottenham Court Road there was, and still is, a Scientology centre. They have people hanging about outside on the pavement trying to entice gullible idiots in. We had nothing much better to do so we all piled in.

They gave us a questionnaire each to fill in. And the results really showed the four different characters in the band. Well, three different characters really because Steve and Paul always kind of lumped themselves together. They were like Fred Flintstone and Barney Rubble, that's how I used to think of them.

I went into another room to talk to a Scientology person. He started telling me that I was an emotional cretin and to improve I'd have to pay them a load of money to get into their reading room — at £10 an hour. I said, hang on a minute, you haven't even read my questionnaire yet. I filled it in. You're telling me all this guff and you haven't even read what I wrote. I thought it was all a joke, you've really got to be some schmuck to fall for that one. And I walked out.

I hung around outside, waiting. After a few minutes, Fred Flintstone and Barney Rubble emerged. They were really worried. They believed everything they'd been told. Straightaway Steve got on to Malcolm and told him they needed all this money to join up with Scientology. Malcolm told him not to be so stupid.

For ages afterwards all these letters kept arriving at Denmark Street from the Scientologists. They'd say things like, 'Glen, you've been a really naughty boy. You didn't turn up for a meeting two weeks ago.' Malcolm just used to screw them up and chuck them in the bin.

John, however, coined out of it. He conned them into believing he was really into Scientology. So they gave him a job. And, as far as I can remember, he did it. He went up there a couple of times and stood outside on the pavement forcing leaflets on people, trying to get them to come inside. I said to him, don't you think it's morally wrong trying to con people like that, getting them to shell out all that money? It's exploiting those who are least able to handle it. He said, it's not my fault if people are stupid.

Iggy Pop had a similar attitude. Years later I remember we were recording at Rockfield Studios. We were all eating roast venison and at the same time discussing vegetarianism. Jim (no one who knows him calls him Iggy) being Jim was squatting on the table stuffing everyone else's venison into his roll and eating it with his fingers. The way I see it is this, he said, if animals weren't so stupid, they wouldn't get caught. Just like John.

It was while we were at Denmark Street that the punk scene – as it would later be called – began to develop. All of us would hang around together. Not just The Pistols but others, like Mick Jones – who formed The Clash – and Tony James – who started Generation X.

On Fridays we'd often go to the Royal College of Art where they used to have these great shows which went on till three or four o'clock in the morning. I knew about them because of being at art college and I took Steve and Paul down with me and introduced them to a scene they knew nothing about.

It was after one of those shows that I introduced Mick Jones to Joe Strummer for the first time. A whole crowd of us were walking back to Denmark Street: me and Rat Scabies and Brian James – two founders of The Damned – and Mick Jones and some others. We bumped into Strummer on the corner of Old Compton Street and Frith Street, just down the road from Ronnie Scott's. Which was where Strummer was going.

What you doin'? he said. I went to see this bloke play at Ronnie Scott's last night. He was fucking great. You should go. In fact, he said if I wanted to bring along some mates, he'd get us all in free.

So we checked it out. This being the early days of punk we looked like complete urchins. So everyone working on the door at Ronnie's had a good laugh at us while Strummer was hustling to get us in. Tom said if I brought some mates, he'd get us in.

Tom who? said the bloke on the door.

Tom Waits.

Oh, he said, but he did go off and fetch him.

And there was Tom Waits at the door, in this big Crombie coat. Hey Joe! What can I do for you?

Well, you said if I brought a couple of mates down, you'd get us in.

Yeah, that should be OK. How many of you are there?

We had a quick count up and there were about 10 of us. Hey! said Tom, hang on there a minute.

He leant back against the door, opened this big overcoat and there, in the inside pocket, was a pint of Guinness with a perfect head on it.

He can't have put it there for effect because he didn't know who was going to be there. He just *happened* to have a pint of Guinness with a perfect head on it in his pocket. How he managed it I don't know. I've tried to do it endless times since but the drink just goes everywhere.

He stood there, reached into the coat, pulled out the pint, drank it all down in one go and nodded to the barman. Hey! Let the boys in.

And he was great.

Another person who was around the scene at the time was Chrissie Hynde who, after Malcolm's shop and writing for the *NME*, had really been scuffling around. One night I remember, she knocked on the door at Denmark Street just as we were packing up.

The other guys all left and she walked out with me. As we got to Tottenham Court Road–which is just round the corner–she spotted the Ann Summers sex shop there and said, hang on, let's just pop in there for a minute. What are you going in there for? I said. To get a job.

It wasn't that she wanted to work in a sex shop but that she needed work of some kind. She'd been writing for the *NME*, about David Cassidy and things like that, but it must have been quite a struggle to get by. She was an alien in the country and she didn't have much money. So basically she was looking for a job. Still, even though they didn't need any staff, I must admit I thought Ann Summers was a funny one to pick.

Paul was a big problem for a while. John and I were on the dole. Steve got by as best he knew how. But Paul had a full-time job. We were always putting pressure on him to jack it in. We told him that this was a band for full-timers not part-timers.

He was an apprentice electrician at Watneys brewery. As he'd nearly finished his apprenticeship, he was understandably loathe to pack it in. He must have reckoned that having a back-up trade was always a handy thing when you're going into something as risky as the music business. My dad certainly agreed with him. He was always on at me to become a cab driver or something. Just in case the music didn't work out.

But Paul didn't like to admit that this was the reason he didn't want to give up his day job. So he created a smokescreen, making the excuse that he didn't think Steve was a good enough guitarist by himself and that we needed a second guitar. Nothing but a diversionary tactic.

So we had to go through a whole charade of auditioning a second guitarist. We put an ad in the *Melody Maker* which read: Whizz Kid Guitarist. Not older than 20. Not worse looking than Johnny Thunders. Auditioning. Tin Pan Alley. Ring 351 0764, 673 0855.

All these Herberts turned up. The first bloke was late so,

instead of waiting, we decided to go to the pub. Just as we were leaving he turned up in the hallway.

He was Greek or something like that. Definitely a bit of a bubble. He had snakeskin boots and a matching snakeskin guitar case. His shirt was undone to the waist, showing off a little gold shark's tooth on a chain and a Keith Richards-style scarf. With him was a friend dressed exactly the same.

We walked straight past, pretending not to notice him, but he got hold of Malcolm and said, where's the audition?

You can't be for the audition, said Malcolm.

Why do you think that? said Mr Snakeskin.

Well, said Malcolm, did you read the ad?

Yes.

Well, you must have missed the bit where it said 'not worse looking than Johnny Thunders.' The poor bloke was completely crestfallen.

But it was mostly all like that. People turn up for auditions who can't play at all. You get used to it. The only one who really could play was Steve New who was later in The Rich Kids with me.

He turned up for the audition with his art teacher, Rose, who he was dating at the time. He told us he was 16 but really he was only 15.

Him apart, though, it was pretty much all no-hopers – nothing more than a total waste of time and a convenient way for Paul to take the pressure off himself. So we took Steve New on as second guitarist.

But he was on a hiding to nothing really. Jonesy was getting better by the minute on the guitar and the sound we were after had no space for the flash lead work that Steve could play so well. So, after a month with two guitarists, we were back to being what we started out to be, a four-piece.

7

TIN PAN
Alley

a lot of people, then and now, have said we couldn't play. The fuck we couldn't. That was an idea that Malcolm pushed hard after I left, trumpeting away with it in *The Great Rock 'n' Roll Swindle*, and telling anyone who'd listen that he was the real Sex Pistol and he couldn't play – so therefore being able to play was quite irrelevant.

We could play well. We could set up a steady groove and keep blasting away all night as hard as life. Listen to the live bootlegs which have come out over the years and you'll hear a lot of it is certainly accomplished. Sometimes it's a bit noisy and something of a racket but that was the intention. You can always hear the real, conscientious effort that went into writing a song and performing it.

Take 'Pretty Vacant', the only song I wrote entirely by myself. The first idea for it came from a poster that Malcolm had brought back from the States, a small handbill for a Richard Hell Television gig with the titles of several songs scattered across it.

One of the songs was '(The Arms Of) Venus De Milo'. Another was '(I Belong To The) Blank Generation'. Both songs said that somewhere something pretty fundamental was missing. As soon as I saw that I thought: that's the kind of feeling that we want to get across in our songs.

Not long after that I was sitting around during a sound-check at The Nashville. I was wondering what to do with this Blank Generation idea. It certainly summed up how we – and a lot of other people – felt at the time. There was a blank, vacant kind of feeling going around which pervaded the scene. Glam rock was exhausted and nothing had come along to replace it. How could I express that feeling in a distinctly Sex Pistols way?

As I was thinking this through, John was doing his sound-check. They were testing out the stage lights at the same time and he was covered with this horrible green light which looked even worse on top of his orange hair. God, I thought, he looks pretty awful.

And the two words came together. Pretty awful plus blank and vacant equalled 'Pretty Vacant'. Also I could immediately see it as a bit of a joke on John. I could imagine him standing there with the green light all over him singing 'We're so pretty, we're so pretty.'

The Blank Generation idea also linked to discussions we'd been having around the band. There was a lot of talk around that time about nihilism and dadaism. Some of the music press stories on us stressed that aspect quite heavily. And I'd come across some of it doing my reading for the 20th-century art section of my art college foundation course.

So what I was trying to do was take those kind of ideas and make them really simple. Use the idea but strip it right down to the bone. From the beginning, the important thing was to get across the *idea* of the band in the songs of the band. We had to turn meaning into sound.

So I wrote the lyrics to 'Pretty Vacant' – all of which are mine, apart from a couple of lines that John later changed in the second verse. I wrote something along the lines of 'If you don't like this, up your bum, we're going down the pub.' John changed it to, 'Forget your cheap comments, we know we're for real.' Which is a far, far better lyric. But the crux of the song is mine.

Yet, although I quickly wrote a tune of sorts, it was never quite right. What I needed was one particular musical idea which would echo the lyrical idea.

Finally that riff came to me in Moonies, an upstairs bar in Charing Cross Road, across the street from The Cambridge Theatre. I was in there one lunchtime drinking my way through that week's dole money when Abba's 'SOS' came on the jukebox.

I heard the riff on it, one simple repeated octave pattern. All I did was take that pattern and alter it slightly – putting in the fifth, to be technical. Got it, I thought. What could be simpler? I'm the Marcel Duchamp of the fretboard, creating my own ready-mades.

The next stage was to fit that Abba riff to the chord sequence for the chorus. That came straight from The Small Faces' 'Wham Bam, Thank You Ma'am' because it fitted so well.

One not so obvious point about the song is this: it's a very simple song in terms of its construction and if you're going to be simple, you should be as simple as you possibly can. 'Boredom' by The Buzzcocks is a perfect example of that. The one-note guitar solo expresses exactly what the song is about. So the simple riff is the very centre of 'Pretty Vacant'. It establishes the basic idea and feeling of the song. We could have sat around playing really fiddly chords. If we'd applied ourselves in that direction, we would have been quite capable of doing it. But we didn't, we deliberately chose to go our own way, keeping it as basic as possible.

I'm amazed that no one has yet noticed that 'Pretty Vacant' is borrowed from 'SOS'. But that's what songwriting is all about. Everything is nicked from something else. Only later, years after you've written the song, do you usually let on.

The trick of it is always the same, to make it sound original. But that, of course, is the hard part. For instance, you take a hook but then make it more interesting by playing around with it in rehearsal. You'll shift it here and there to fit the confines of a particular song's structure. By the time you've done all that, if you've done it well, it will sound like your own idea. Originality through larceny.

'Pretty Vacant' was one of the first real songs we wrote. It was our standard bearer before 'Anarchy' and 'God Save The Queen', both of which were only written nearly a year later. At that time we were mostly still playing cover versions. But that was also another way we established our identity.

We'd work out which songs we ought to cover by kicking ideas around in the pub. Anybody was allowed to chip in. Sometimes Bernie would offer ideas, sometimes Jamie Reid. It was a collective consciousness. Key words would get bandied around, in-vogue words like nihilism, and themes and attitudes would be assessed. A whole evening's conversation would be devoted to what constitutes being 'actionary' as opposed to 'reactionary'. The funny thing is that for all this talk, it was always the band who had to push to get anything done – let's see this 'action' – because talk would have been all that remained. Bernard was incorrigible; he'd talk the hind legs off a donkey and then discuss why it wouldn't budge. From there, though, we'd find songs which would express an idea.

When we were casting around for songs we also had to bear in mind our limits. When Wally had been given his cards Steve had to struggle to cover all the guitar work by himself. He couldn't play complex signatures or flash lead lines – not that we'd have wanted either – so that dictated the simplicity of our sound. Simple and loud.

We had to look for songs by people whose work fitted the bill, whose songs we had a good chance of being able to play as a unit. Naturally we turned to The Who, The Small Faces, people like that, doing 'Substitute', 'Understanding' and The Monkees' 'Steppin' Stone'.

John had a few ideas in that direction. He brought in 'Psychotic Reaction' by The Count Five, an original sixties American punk song, and 'Thru My Eyes', a dreadful psychedelic dirge which we soon elbowed. From somewhere someone came up with a very early tape of Jonathan Richman – this is a couple of years before he had a record out – and we'd play his 'Roadrunner'.

Sometimes we'd take a trip up to a record stall in Gold-bourne Road, Ted Carroll's, and go through the stacks of sin-gles looking for songs with ideas. Once I picked up a load of Kinks records. We thought of doing their 'I'm Not Like Any-body Else'. Then everybody around our scene started playing it. Mick Jones' band were doing it. Chrissie was playing it. She always had this enormous fascination for The Kinks. Her first record was a Kinks song and she went on to live with a Kink – Ray Davies. In the end, Spedding took 'I'm Not Like Anybody Else', recorded it and used it as the title for one of his albums.

Although we'd started out with a strong Faces influence we gradually became more sophisticated in how we dealt with it. First we reached back to The Small Faces. Then, if I had an interest in something, I read up on it. After a little research, I found out that Ron Wood used to play in a band called The Birds. So I hunted out a Birds record.

After a while Malcolm began to cotton on to what we were doing. He dug out 'Painter Man' by The Creation for us be-cause of their art school connection.

He told us a story about the band, how they would do an action painting on stage while the guitarist was playing a solo, then set fire to the painting. We listened to Malcolm tell the tale and we went off and listened to the record. For a while we were going to do it but somehow it slipped away – which was extremely fortunate when you consider Boney M's subsequent version of it.

That is how a band develops its sound. It's like becoming an actor. You have to do your research to play the role. What you learn then is deeply influential. When you're learning to play this chord rather than that chord because the record you're copying just happens to have that one, then that partic-ular inversion becomes second nature and you think the same way forever after.

Other songs came out of the period when we were rehearsing every day. We would turn up at Denmark Street every day, almost without fail, play for an hour, maybe only half an hour before sloping off. But somebody would always have an idea for something. Every day something new would come through.

We'd filter the ideas, letting the good ones drift through and making sure the naff ones got thrown out. It wasn't a haphazard process.

What separated us from all those second division punk bands – apart from being a good 18 months ahead of them – was the strength of our songs and hooks and the sheer power of it all. Take a band like The Slits. They were trying to do the same kind of thing as us but they didn't succeed, because they couldn't play. At the time there was a general attitude that competence didn't matter. What rubbish. It does.

If you want to get across a powerful idea you have to be able to do it powerfully. You've got to be absolutely solid and spot on. The Pistols might have sometimes sounded like a cacophony but they were always tight, focused. A lot of other up and coming bands missed that simple point.

If you're going to make a point, you've got to be firing on all four cylinders, preferably six. We put a lot of time and effort into ensuring we were.

Like when Malcolm spent a long time in the States, back when Wally was still in the band. People around us were saying, why didn't we get up and play? But we stuck out against that, knowing we weren't ready, it wasn't yet right.

We spent an awful lot of time making sure the whole thing was pared down to the bone, clean as a whistle and really succinct.

'Submission' was another of the early songs to come out of those intensive rehearsals. Before we moved into Denmark Street we did some time at The Roundhouse studio, which is an old railway turntable building in North London.

One day John and I were sitting around in the pub across the road, waiting for Steve and Paul to turn up. We started talking about something Malcolm had been pushing at us. 'Submission', he'd said, that's a good song title. Presumably he thought we should write something about bondage.

I think this bondage idea is a load of cobblers, said John. I agreed. How about this idea? he said, his eyes telling me he had some stroke he was trying to pull. How about a submarine mission?

So we sat and wrote, 'I'm on a submarine mission for you baby/ I could feel the way you were going/ Picked you up on my TV screen/ I could feel your undercurrent flowing.'

And there in those words was the stroke John was pulling. It was a dig at Malcolm about one thing in particular. Malcolm was always taking a pop at him about the way he looked. John looked more than a little Bowieish in those days with his red hair and white face. So Malcolm used to wind him up, saying Ziggy Stardust was all about space whereas John was the exact opposite. Johnny Rotten, Malcolm would say, is the underwater star. So 'Submission' was in part away for John to wind Malcolm up in turn, getting his own back.

Of course, a lot of people have got the idea that neither John nor I wrote any of the lyrics. Some swallowed the lie that Jamie Reid was the band's lyric writer. It's said that he wrote the lyrics to 'Holidays In The Sun'. Considering he'd done most of the artwork for the band and had actually got himself in shtuck for the 'Holidays In The Sun' cover – for borrowing the graphic from some travel company brochure – maybe he did write the lyrics, I don't know. That was one of the very few songs written after I left the band.

But it's also said that he wrote 'Anarchy' and I know that's not true. Perhaps John was round his flat one night and had a chat about anarchy and situationism. Maybe. But as far as I know it was John's lyric.

All I knew of Jamie Reid was that he was a friend of Malcolm's and Sophie Richmond's boyfriend. He was around the scene. Like Bernie he was one of the people who we'd sling ideas around with in the pub. We'd chat with him and you could tell straightaway that he was a seriously political kind of bloke. But it was never the case, as some people have claimed, that

Jamie was the great Situationist thinker, plotting our every move, teaching us what to think and sing.

One thing that a lot of people miss out on is that, as well as his beloved Can and Van Der Graaf Generator, John had a soft spot for Cockney Rebel. And I reckon that might well be where he got at least part of the 'Anarchy' lyric.

On one of the early Cockney Rebel albums there is a section where Steve Harley sings 'dee-stroy'. That's where I think John found that bit. (You always take lyrics from where you can. The words to 'EMI' were partly inspired by an advertising campaign for the Can album, 'Unlimited Edition'.)

When people write about The Pistols they often draw tenuous links with things back in history. But it was all so much more immediate than that. We were kids who were listening to the music of the day. We all had our own little pet bands which took us back a bit into history, but mostly it was solidly contemporary. John, for example, had Van Der Graaf Generator. I had Can, Steve The New York Dolls and Paul Be Bop Deluxe and Roxy Music. The riff in 'No Future' – or 'God Save The Queen' as it came to be known – is directly from the seventies and not the fifties. It's The Spiders From Mars, not Eddie Cochran.

'Anarchy' itself was actually finished right towards the end of the golden period during which John and I were able to work together so well. All that time I'd been coming up with nearly all the musical ideas while John wrote the lyrics.

One day John and I had a chat, deciding that Steve wasn't pulling his weight. He was equally capable of coming up with ideas but he seemed happy to take a back seat. So we gave him a right bollocking at the next rehearsal. But he counter-attacked straight away. Well, he said, you're so fucking clever, what ideas have you got?

All I had was one idea that I'd been kicking around. I picked up the guitar and started to play it – nothing more than just strumming a G chord. But, if you do something with conviction, it can sound like something worth listening to.

Then I added an F and E minor.

So, said Steve, what comes next?

I added a D minor and a C.

I like that, said Steve.

Well, I thought, that's bloody jammy, isn't it?

Paul played a drum pattern. Because we were all working together every day and kicking ideas around we were able to put it into shape very quickly.

John went into a corner and worked on a lyrical idea that he already had. I put together an arrangement – that was my role in the band really, being the arranger, establishing the sound – and we had 'Anarchy In The UK'.

At that stage we would always put the song together there and then, John doing the lyrics on the spot. We'd decide on the tune, work out where the hooks were, where the words were needed and John would do it, maybe polishing it all up a bit later.

There is a story about The Beatles, that every night after a session in the studio they would have a competition to see who could come up with the best ending for the track they were working on by the next morning.

And that is how bands work. You leave something partially finished, then that night you go out to see a band play or listen to something on the radio and, suddenly, there it is, you've found the missing idea. You don't sit there deliberately plagiarising but something you hear often sets off an idea.

Paul's major contribution to the band was attitude. He will never do anything except in his own good time. You can't hurry him to do anything. He has a belligerent attitude which announces, 'I'll do this when I want to do it, no sooner, no later.'

Once people have reached a certain level of proficiency on their instrument they play according to their character. They play as they are. For example, one drummer I worked with called Dave McIntosh, would keep doing really spunky drum fills – that was all his pent-up aggression coming out.

But Paul just wouldn't be hurried. I think that steady rhythm of his was the whole backbone of The Pistols' sound. Everyone thinks that all punk rock was a frenzied, amphetamine sulphate blur, that we all did five-minute sets like Amyl And The Nitrates, but listen to anything by The Pistols and you'll be surprised how slow it is.

There was hardly one fast song among all the material we wrote and recorded. 'Submission' is slow, 'No Feelings' is quite fast and the rest are medium-paced. That all comes down to Paul who was always Mister 'In My Own Good Time'. He was Charlie Watts all over again.

Perhaps we sped up a little when we played live, when the adrenalin aspect of it gets going. But I always felt that when you take your time to play a song it shows your confidence.

A great actor will take the stage gradually and surely, then command it with his presence. He won't rush on, say his lines then rush off again. If he did that it would be like he was embarrassed and in a hurry to get it over with. In our case, Paul provided that stately deliberation.

I'll always remember the time we played Chelmsford Prison, which in those days was a maximum security nick. It was the day Paul finished his apprenticeship at the brewery and he turned up already half-pissed.

Recently, someone gave me a tape of the gig. Listening to it—and we played pretty well that day—two things are immediately noticeable. One, John's effortless rapport with the cons. And two, the sound of Paul falling off his drum stool half-way through the set. Not that he even dropped a beat. Pissed as he was his timing was spot on right through the show.

For some reason, though, nearly all of the other younger punk bands didn't try and copy us but the New York band, The Ramones and their speed thrash. The Ramones had got it together before us and developed in parallel to us but although The Pistols had all trooped along together to check out their London debut at Dingwalls, we really didn't feel we had that much in common with them. We considered them more of a comedy band. I always reckoned the reason all those other bands copied The Ramones was because they couldn't afford that much rehearsal time so they had to hurry through their set and finish it before they got slung out of their rehearsal rooms.

As Paul wouldn't be hurried, so Steve approached everything in a really ham-fisted manner. He took the most simple idea and kept on and on at it until the point was taken. Which meant all the way through our songs. And that very simple approach worked fine. It gave our sound real cohesion and made us sound quite different from anyone else.

And Steve was exactly the same in his daily life. He'd get hold of an expression and never let it go. 'Corry' was one of his favourites for a while. I've no idea what it really means but he used it to indicate a girl's private parts. For at least a month, every time a girl walked past, he'd go, cor, look at the corry on that! Or, cor, that's a corry! Or, cor, get that corry!

For that whole month it would seem like that was the only thing he could say. He'd get one idea in his head at a time and batter away at it until it died of exhaustion.

Different songs were written in different ways. 'Problems' came out one afternoon when we were all bored, sitting around thinking, what are we going to do now? I played a little riff. Steve added something more, a Faces kind of rhythm in the bridge. That song was a real four-way thing.

'God Save The Queen' I wrote while we were in the studio working on 'Anarchy'. I was fiddling around at the piano between takes when I got the idea for the musical part of it. I really worked it out then presented it to them as a more or less finished tune.

The idea came from 'Pushin' And Shovin' (Don't Give Me No Lip Child)', the Dave Berry song we played in the early days. There was something of that in the riff, and there was also a funky element which came from my being impressed by Paul Riley, the bass player in Roogalator, who we supported at our second-ever gig, at the Central School of Art.

But the guitar riff I came up with, with sixes and sevens in it, was something of a struggle for Steve. His style was more rock 'n' roll, all major chords and fifths.

While we were waiting for him to get his fingers round the part, John and I left the Denmark Street room and went for something to eat in the Giaconda, a couple of doors along. Two jam puddings and custard later we trooped back to find Steve had learned to play it. But the way he'd taught himself to do it was all wrong. His fingers were in the wrong places. Instead of playing a sixth and a seventh, he was playing a thirteenth and an eleventh – which is basically just playing it on the wrong strings. But it sounded great, so we went with it.

That could come about only because we put ourselves in the position of rehearsing every day. We were very strict about it, which meant the ideas came through. A real sixties kind of workshop thing.

But after 'Pretty Vacant' I found it very hard to write a lyric. For me that encapsulated everything we were about. It was, 'We're pretty vacant and we don't care, so fuck you, pal.'

By then it had also become a bit of a battlefield between John and me, so I was quite happy for him to write all the lyrics. We'd written 'Submission' together and we'd worked together on what eventually became 'New York'. But mainly it was a case of my bringing a tune I'd worked on into a rehearsal where we would arrange it. Then John would sit down and write some lyrics.

He's a great lyricist. His words are very descriptive. He can set something up so clearly in just one line. Like, 'Down in the pit where the typewriter blips,' in 'I Wanna Be Me'.

In an interview he can talk an absolute load of twaddle but it's always fantastic copy. His songs are like that too. 'Bodies', for instance. It's a great song, but at the end of it you're no wiser as to whether it's pro or anti abortion.

Our negative stance was deliberate and we tried to make sure it ran right through all our songs. Paul brought 'Steppin' Stone' to us and I'm sure the main reason we all liked it was that it was negative, that it was I'm *not* your steppin' stone.

Basically we were always looking for songs with 'no' in the title. I once went through the set list and everything was so anti. I thought, how can we be this nihilistic? It was, No Lip, No Feelings, No Fun, No Future – which was what 'God Save The Queen' was called at that time. Anything with 'no' in the title and that was for us.

8

Punk's First SUMMER

the summer of 1976 was long and hot. Just as the hippies had come out of the warmth of the summer of love so punks came out of this scorcher. Warm evenings really changed London. The atmosphere was less British than New Orleans-like. It was as if you were on the set of *Cat On A Hot Tin Roof* or *A Streetcar Named Desire*. Normally Londoners live very isolated lives, but because of the heat people were hanging out on street corners a lot more. And, if you're still living at home with your parents, you just want to get out more than ever.

It was during that summer we really started to be followed by the Bromley Contingent—Siouxsie Sioux, Steve Severin, Billy Idol and the others. They'd been coming into the shop quite often, much as John had.

But the main reason they became such fervent followers was, I think, because very early on we played a gig at Ravensbourne College of Art in South London. Which was as good as Bromley as far as they were concerned. They felt, I think, that us playing Bromley was a local equivalent of the star appearing in the East. There was no intention on our part, it just worked out that way, but from that day on they were at nearly every gig. We became an excuse for them all to go out together, rather like people who will go and see their football team wherever they happen to be playing.

A lot of people somehow seem to have got the idea that they were hooligans, always fighting. Nothing could be further from the truth. Like all early Pistols fans – except maybe Sid Vicious – they came from an arty background and were never into popping people. Their idea of a good night out was making sure everyone was extremely impressed by what they were wearing.

We got quite friendly with them. Billy Idol was still William Broad in the beginning. He was very quiet in those days. Not that any of them dressed particularly outrageously – that came later – but Billy was always the least outrageous. He was very Bill Brown, like anyone you'd meet in a saloon bar.

One story sums Billy up for me. I'd run into him at the Red Cow, a dump of a gig in Hammersmith. Two girls were with him but, despite the way his eyes ran over them all evening, they weren't thinking along the same lines as him.

There's a party, he said, fancy coming? Follow me then.

1 didn't even know he had a car. But there outside the pub was a spanking new Austin Princess. They'd only just come on the market and this was a top of the range number in British racing green.

So I hopped in my beat-up old car and started to follow him. Instead of poodling along carefully at 30 miles an hour Billy – to impress the pair of girls he'd got on the back seat – started slashing across London like he was Ayrton Senna.

Up past Kensington, round Shepherd's Bush roundabout, he tried to lose me. He hared up Holland Park Avenue, down Ladbroke Grove and up to the junction at the Great Western Road.

And then we came to the hump-backed bridge. When I got to the brow I realised I was in trouble. A car trying to turn right hadn't left enough room for Billy to squeeze through. He'd come to a stop. And I had to slam on my brakes. Unfortunately I'd just had them fixed that week. If I hadn't I'd have shuddered to a stop. As it was they locked.

I smashed right into the back of Billy's car. He jumped straight out, almost in tears.

Look what you've done, he kept saying, look what you've done. This car, this car, it's my dad's car. He's gone away for the week, it's brand new and he said, on no account must I use it, I mustn't even touch the keys.

As he was saying this the girls thanked him for the lift and tootled off to get a cab.

The smash cost me £350 in the end but it was very nearly worth every penny to see the look on Billy's face when he had to admit it was his dad's car.

I remember going to a party at Siouxsie's house in Bromley. Her parents must have been away. We turned up and she answered the door in nothing but one of those plastic aprons with suspenders and stockings printed on it, the kind of thing you might give your mother-in-law as a joke Christmas present. Well, we thought, this looks quite interesting. It was. Steve and our roadie went through most of the birds, one after another, while I sloped off with my girlfriend.

The reason the Bromley Contingent became famous is that the name kept on being knocked around at the very time that people were looking for a movement. Bernie and Malcolm were pushing the idea of a punk movement from their end. And journalists like Caroline Coon, who wrote for the *Melody Maker*, and John Ingham of *Sounds* were keen on using it to make their mark. So people thought that the Bromley Contingent were a group. As their fame grew, the same question kept coming up: do they have a record out yet?

I don't know for certain, but I wouldn't be at all surprised if Malcolm hadn't hatched up a plot with Bernie. They could well have figured that both their bands could gain the most momentum if they made it look like a big happening movement. But we didn't have a pack running behind us, apart from Bernie's band which wasn't off the ground yet. So Malcolm and Bernie got the idea that they could court journalists and convince them there was a movement. It was in the writers' interest to forsake a journalistic stance in favour of a fan club one. They were as keen as anyone for it to work. It all became one big, self-fulfilling prophecy.

Take what happened with Louise's. It was a dyke club in Poland Street where we – and the Bromley Contingent – used to hang out sometimes. As much as anything else it was another example of Malcolm's desire to belong to as many different clubs and underground societies as he could.

Apart from the slightly interesting idea of hanging out with all these dykes I didn't see much more to it. Yet, by the time Louise's became processed through the press, it was seen as being so important you might think punk was invented there. When really it was just an average drinker full of the Chagueramas crowd.

We played a lot of gigs that summer. In fact, we played a good portion of all The Sex Pistols gigs there ever were. We played several times at The Nashville Rooms in West London. At the time it was still the centre of the tail end of pub rock.

The first time we played there was when we acquired the services of Dave Goodman – who later became the producer of our first, unreleased version of 'Anarchy' – and his partner, Kim Thraves. Dave just happened to be doing the sound for us that night because he owned the PA we'd hired. He was so knocked out by us that he asked if he could do our sound full-time – which was handy for us as we got a soundman, a PA and a van all in one swoop.

The night was meant to be a co-headline with Joe Strummer's band, The 101ers, but we went on first. Great, said Steve, more time to pull the birds. And he had a point. One of the worst things about playing clubs in England is you finish the gig and say, right let's have a drink. But the bar's shut. Any other country in the world and the bands are treated like kings. Here the attitude is, fuck off now you're finished.

We did well at The Nashville. Malcolm might not have known much about the mechanics of management but he certainly knew how to cut a deal. The last show we played there he completely stitched them up. They had to give us 100 percent of the door money, plus they had to provide the PA and us with drinks. All they got to keep was what was left of the bar takings. Malcolm really enjoyed that.

But the Nashville show everyone remembers is the one where a fight broke out. At the time the papers gave the impression that we started the fight but that just wasn't true. We tried to stop it, in fact.

It was all Vivienne's fault. She'd taken a seat in front of the stage and, when she went off to get a drink, some bloke just sat down in her seat not knowing it was hers. When she came back with her drink she wanted her seat back.

You can't reserve seats here, he said. And got jumped for his pains. Because it was Vivienne, all the kids who hung out in the shop joined in on her side. I felt really sorry for the poor bloke because he was getting a right hammering. It was something like eight on one. Even Malcolm joined in—like some action man, leaping over people's shoulders to get his punches in. Sid was caught steaming in by a photographer. You can see real madness in his eyes in that picture. The retinas look like they're on fire as he 'defends' Vivienne.

And, as the fight began, we're starting to play. As far as we were concerned it was a clear case of Vivienne being her usual cantankerous, contrary self. We could see the bloke getting a right pasting and we just thought: Vivienne's starting trouble again.

Mostly, we were annoyed. For a simple basic reason—whenever there's a fight in a crowd you lose whatever rapport you might have built up with them. A fight is always more interesting to watch than the band.

So we jumped off stage—not to join in but to stop it. At least I did. Steve maybe was after a bundle. But this poor bloke was getting a hammering for nothing when it was Vivienne who really deserved a sock in the mouth.

And, when it did hit the papers, we didn't—as some people seem to have thought—revel in the publicity. We were worried. We didn't think: great, we're all over the papers. We thought it might ruin our career.

We did gigs all round the country that summer. At a gig

in North Allerton, Derbyshire, to our surprise there were two punk rockers in the audience. They turned out to be Pauline Murray and her boyfriend, who shortly after went on to form Penetration and have a minor hit with 'Come Into The Open'. Their appetite had been whetted by early reports in the music papers. This was their first opportunity to take a look-see and they certainly dressed for the occasion, sticking right out from all the other chicken-in-the-basket cases. The compère announced us. Tonight, ladies and gentlemen, we present the debut up North of Sex Pistol in cabaret.

In Whitby, the fishing port, we played upstairs in a working men's club. After two numbers, a man came in and waved us to stop. I'm sorry boys, he said, but it's no good. We've had a meeting of the committee and we've decided you can't go on any longer. We'll still pay you, of course, but at the moment we can't hear the bingo being called.

At The Rock Garden, Middlesborough, we supported The Doctors Of Madness who were a supposedly shocking group knocking around then. They reneged on their promise to let us use their PA. Steve was so furious that he gobbed in their stage boots when they weren't looking, so they had to go on stage with their feet squelching in his spit.

Then he picked up this Yorkshire scrubber, who was about as tasty as a cold fried egg. He disappeared beneath the stage with her during the Doctors' set. Where have you been? we said when he came out. Well, he said, they've all got holes, ain't they?

For all those out of town shows we'd travel up in Dave Goodman's Transit van. There'd be seven of us stuffed in it – the band plus Dave and Kim and Nils, all our gear and the PA. Although to begin with we were only getting paid £25 per gig that crept up fairly rapidly over the summer. Soon we were getting £50 to £60 a show.

The idea of doing all these shows was to turn us into a real live band, get the groundwork done, and get our name known around the country. The same reasons any young band tears up and down motorways in an over-full Transit. Or rather *did*;

these days bands don't tour till after the hit single, the hit album and half a dozen videos.

For one Scottish gig John, Paul and I travelled separately from the rest of them. We took the train up while Steve went in the van. The gig was wild. We literally got bottled offstage. We ran to the dressing room which was directly behind the stage and hid as the bottles cracked against the door. No one's idea of fun. Later we got talking to a couple of locals in the bar. We only threw the bottles, they said, because we heard you liked that kind of thing.

But the hotel for that show was great. Frankie Vaughan was staying there at the same time and, for the first time in our lives, we got to order from room service. What with the opportunity for us to tuck into six different kinds of fish for breakfast it was a long time before we were allowed to order from room service again.

We also played at The Lyceum in London, supporting The Pretty Things on an all-night bill. Back to square one! We learned some hard lessons about how you have to pace yourself a bit. Normally when you go for a drink you have a few beers and then, at 11 o'clock, they sling you out. So you get used to that kind of drinking schedule.

At an all-nighter you can just keep going. And we did. Come one o'clock in the morning you've got to go on stage and all that booze really doesn't make for a good gig. When we went on John staggered across the stage and stubbed out a cigarette on his hand–for effect.

When I thought about it later I decided it was really impressive but at the time I was pissed and all I remember thinking was, what's John doing with a fag in his hand when he doesn't even smoke?

This was when punk rock, although we hated that phrase at the time, really started becoming a movement. A lot of the new bands used to come and practise in Denmark Street. Mick Jones came down with Bernie once when he and Tony James (later of Generation X and Sigue Sigue Sputnik) were trying to get London 55 together. At one stage or another the London

55 included practically everyone outside The Pistols' camp who went on to achieve anything on the punk rock scene and plenty that didn't.

They all trooped in looking like horrendous New York Dolls clones in stack-heeled boots six inches high. Mick had a see-through shirt on and his ears were sticking right through his long, lank hair. Later, when we were looking for a second guitarist in the band, Mick came down and played with us, but at first our reaction was, the state of them! We thought they were meant to be getting it together with something original like us! What is Malcolm on about? What is Bernie doing with them? Yet despite his appalling dress sense, Mick soon became a good friend.

Other people would come down. I'd play bass with Mick on guitar and Steve Jones on drums – he was a good drummer actually, real solid sense of rhythm – while Mick was trying out Chrissie Hynde for his band. Chrissie had a strange song she was working on which sounded like The Kinks' 'Sittin' On Your Sofa' and was called 'Get On Your Hynde Legs, Baby'.

Joe Strummer I met at The Acklam Hall, just before one of the shows at The Nashville. Joe's band, The 101ers, were supporting us, so Steve and I went down to see him play the night before, to check him out. We went backstage and crept up on him humming while he was tuning his guitar, trying to put him off. He turned round. So, he said, Sex Pistols are you? We'll see tomorrow night.

Which I suppose he did, as it was not long after that he jacked in The 101ers, cut his hair and joined Mick and Bernie to put The Clash together.

We were close to The Clash in those early days – partly because of Bernie's friendship with Malcolm, partly because of mine with Mick. They played their first gig supporting us, at the Black Swan in Sheffield, and they played their first public gig in London with us, at the Screen on the Green cinema in Islington.

This was in the period when we were finding it very difficult to get gigs. It wasn't that people didn't want to see us.

It was that the 'mafia' of London's club owners didn't want to let us play.

Malcolm was a mate of the bloke who ran the Screen on the Green. They knew each other from the shop and Malcolm knew the cinema well as he'd often catch a late night movie there. When Malcolm asked if we could play there, he was told it was OK but there were two problems: one, it would have to be after the last show and two, as there was no stage we would have to provide our own.

We got round that by dumping it in The Clash's lap. They wanted to support us so we agreed on the condition that they built the stage. Fine, they said, we'll provide a stage. No, we said, *build* it, and put all the posters up. That, we thought, was teaching them their place. Malcolm saw it as a chance to have a go at Bernie.

When we were getting ready for the show Dave Goodman turned up with a surprise for us. Here, he said, I've got these bombs for you, they'll go off during the set, big flash, big bang, be great.

Get out of it, we told him, that's fucking hippy shit, Pink Floyd have those, we don't want to know.

Are you sure? he said. It's a really good idea.

We're sure.

OK then, sure?

Sure.

On we went. Halfway through 'Anarchy'–our *first* number–and BANG! Wallop. What the fuck's that?

Dave had broken his promise. Not only that, one of the bombs fell over and set fire to a curtain. So we had to stand there playing away as if nothing had happened while someone ran for a fire extinguisher before the whole place burned down.

Then John knocked his tooth against the mike, losing the cap and having to scrabble around the stage looking for it. Meanwhile Siouxsie decided to get on stage and flash her tits. It was a good night all round.

The 100 Club, of course, is where we really started to cement our reputation. The first show there was nearly empty but, by the last time we played there, the place was full hours before we went on stage.

Despite the heat of that summer I wore a rubber suit from Malcolm's shop, a jeans suit with zip pockets on the seat with nothing behind them. Undo the zip and your bum showed through.

I was so naive about gigging that I didn't even think to bring a change of clothes. So, after playing a show, jumping around in a basement packed to the gills, I'd go directly from the stage to try and catch the last tube home to my girlfriend's place in Putney.

I'd stand on the platform dripping with sweat. I had a pair of red slingback suede shoes at the time and the sweat would run down the inside of the rubber trousers – real drainpipes – come out at the cuffs and spread in a large puddle around the shoes. All because I didn't know enough to take a change of clothes.

Sniffin' Glue, the punk fanzine, started that summer, during the time we were packing out The 100 Club. Caroline Coon, the journalist, introduced me to Mark P., who'd just started it up with Danny Baker.

He's a young journalist, she said, just like you're a young musician. Really patronising. I looked at Mark P. and thought, who is this fucking prat?

He showed me a tattered sheaf of papers he had in his hand – called The Bible or something – and I realised he had no idea of what we were about. One big thought flashed through my head, the idea of all these people trying to get on the bandwagon, missing the point because they made it look so tacky and cheap.

The whole point of The Pistols was a question of style. Compare us with The Clash, say. We were always far more stylish. Our clothes came from Malcolm's shop and we always had the best of everything.

All our gear was nicked but it was the finest gear. Our mikes were stolen from Bowie at the Hammersmith Odeon and they were the best mikes you could get.

(Years later I got to talk about that with Bowie himself, while I was rehearsing with Iggy Pop. Bowie tried hard to write off the whole punk movement as nothing more than the 'noble savage'. I reminded him of the stolen mikes and pointed out he'd written a song with the line which ran, 'The bitter comes out better on a stolen guitar.' Touché.)

Steve and Paul had always had the attitude that nothing but the best was good enough for them. That stretched right back to the early days. When I first auditioned with them I turned up at Wally's place with a 25 quid Hofner bass, a right state it was. Call that a guitar? they said, play this, and they gave me a practically new Fender Precision bass.

Which is part of the reason we fought so hard against being called punks. To us punk was a loser term and we didn't want to be thought of as losers.

Caroline Coon would call us punks and we'd say, we're not fucking punks, let those Herberts The Clash be punks. We always saw ourselves as above the rest of them, all those second division bands like 999. But without them, of course, you wouldn't have had a movement. So, in so far as it furthered our aims, we tolerated it.

Everyone copied us because it was the easiest thing to do. When we said we wanted there to be a hundred bands like us we didn't mean a hundred bands copying us, we meant a hundred bands with our originality and sense of style.

But the second division bands didn't have the range of influences we did. We were their influences. They saw our rough edges and mistakes and took them as gospel.

They didn't see what John took from Van Der Graaf Generator. They didn't see what John and I took from Can. They didn't see any of the things which gave what we did its quality and depth. All they saw was the facade and they merely copied it.

It was also in that long hot summer of 1976 that John really began to change. For the first three months he was in the band, he and I got on like a house on fire. We did a hell of a lot of work, writing and polishing the songs. Then the rot set in.

Quite why that happened I don't know, although later there was the problem of what happened when he got some press. Quite simply his head got bigger with every article— which might sound like sour grapes but I honestly don't think it is.

One strange thing about him that I could never understand was how he could never ever go anywhere by himself. There was always an entourage. He couldn't even take a piss by himself.

You could never be by yourself with John. There was always someone else you'd have to deal with, be it John Grey or Jah Wobble or Sid. (The reason for the nicknames, by the way, was that they were all named John.)

John's friends were more than a bit strange. Take Wobble, for instance. One day he turned up at Denmark Street to meet John after rehearsals. Sorry I'm late, he said, but I got stopped by this copper.

Yeah?

So I killed him, said Wobble, his eyes glazing over.

First I punched him and he went down. Then I got my knife out and stabbed him. But he was still groaning so I got my machine gun out and gave him a few quick bursts. That got the fucker.

And John accepted all that. The rest of us, of course, looked at each other as if to say, what have we got on our hands here? Then got our arses out of the building double quick.

Maybe John always had his entourage because he was the last one to join the band, the last one on the boat. Perhaps he felt he needed the security of his own gang. But I thought it was crazy when he'd turn up for rehearsals with someone like John Grey. You don't take your mate to work with you. Imagine turning up for your shift at the pie factory and you've got your mate with you. It's just not on.

And John Grey in particular would always stick his oar in. There were enough of us sticking our oars in already. I think that was when I started falling out with him. His entourage was just an unnecessary diversion. And sometimes it was more than that. One time, a few days after I'd come up with the song, I was telling John Grey about writing 'Pretty Vacant' and how pleased I was with it, although I wasn't fully happy with my lyrics for the second verse and maybe John could do something there. What do you mean? said John Grey. John wrote the whole song, he told me so. Gossip like that you really don't need.

In the early days, though, we'd go out together sometimes when we'd finished writing, see a few gigs, have a few beers. A couple of times I ended up staying at his mum's place in Finsbury Park.

We'd go and see some wretched rockabilly band like Brent Ford And The Nylons at an art school where we'd tuck back the cheap wine or Newcastle Brown at 30 pence a bottle. Which doesn't do your head much good the next day. Imagine waking up with the most horrendous hangover and being greeted by one of John's brothers and sisters saying, who's this on the sofa then? to their mum as she got ready for work.

It was also at his mum's house that I found out what a liar he is. I think he's a truly terrible liar but I always figured there were two ways of looking at it.

One, you think, good on him because he manages to get away with it. Or two, he's living the kind of lie that Jean Cocteau wrote about in *Thomas The Imposter*, the story of a man who lies his way through life. He rises to being a general by lying. But, because he's a general, he ends up being shot.

John would always say, I hate eating and I refuse to eat, I'll only eat lettuce. And that's what he'd do. But this night we'd been out on the piss and as soon as we got back to his place he was straight into the kitchen, straight into the cupboard and stuffing his face.

Unless I'd gone to his house I'd never have known he was lying about not eating. He'd said he didn't eat so often that I started thinking, well, maybe it's true, he is very thin in the face, maybe he really doesn't eat anything except lettuce.

John really started to change once he'd had his name in the papers but it began as early as when we were writing 'Submission'. Before that he'd always been, well not pleasant but civil at least.

We were upstairs at Denmark Street, arguing over whether the chorus in 'Submission' should come after the second verse or after the bridge. I was basically winning the argument when he turned round to me and said, drop dead.

There's no answer to that, I thought, and ignored him. A stony silence and what seemed like half an hour later, he turned round and said, you're still here. The look on his face told me that he really believed somehow that if he told me to drop dead, I would. Oh well, I thought, John really has gone a bit doolally now.

You just had to put up with a constant tirade of bullshit from John. Total lies and denial. He'd say something and two minutes later he'd completely deny he'd ever said it. To an outsider that could seem quite amusing. If you're trying to do a job of work with the man it's just not on. He could take denial to quite extraordinary lengths. One example was the night we supported Screaming Lord Sutch in High Wycombe. Being a generous sort, Sutch allowed us to use his PA.

We went on stage facing maybe 1500 people – and right away we realised there was something seriously wrong with the sound coming out of the monitors. It was absolutely diabolical. And we knew who was to blame. Steve Hayes and Jim, two mates of Steve and Paul's, who had taken it upon themselves to be our sound men for the night. Their qualifications were impeccable. Steve was a carpenter and Jim was a plasterer. That night they were both plastered.

Unable to hear himself sing, John – in full view of the audience – vented his frustration by smashing each vocal mike in turn, then smashing a couple of the equipment mikes for good measure.

Bang, our set came to a sudden halt. And there were Sutch's band ready to kick our heads in for smashing up what, after all, was their gear.

John denied everything. He denied even denting a mike. The fact that 1500 people had seen him smash up five mikes didn't faze him at all. He denied he'd so much as scratched any of them.

And he got away with it. For reasons I could never fathom, Sutch thought it was all incredibly funny and let him off.

Not only that. Ron Watts was the promoter of the gig. He thought we were interesting and booked us into the gig he ran in London, The 100 Club.

But I never understood why John had to be like that. So I wouldn't put up with it. I'd fight back. I was never content to be nothing more than the bass player who does what he's told. I came up with a lot of musical ideas so I felt I had a right to be heard.

But quite honestly John often seemed more interested in coming up with power plays than anything else. Which is the kind of thing that happens everywhere, in every office, in every business, in every football team. But when there's just four of you everything becomes that much more concentrated.

I still think that if I was a sage and 999 years old and had experienced all manner of horrors and learned how to deal with them and tolerate them, even if I'd been through all that, I still don't think I'd be able to deal with John being as contrary as he is.

It's total self-promotion for him. Which is fine if that's the game you're going to play. But what I could never come to terms with was the fact that he carried on like that in private. Have the snottiest public persona imaginable, that's OK. But don't keep it up off stage. Don't shit on your workmates— which is what John did.

And, of course, he was only able to get away with it because of his public status. In the normal scheme of things, amongst your own niche of people—the small clan of workmates or family we all have—if you acted like John did, nobody would put up with it. You'd be ostracised or have your head kicked in or be treated like the village idiot.

But fame has its own mechanics. So John got away with it. Of course, his support crew, the Rotten entourage, made it easier for him. And later it was compounded by the arrival of Nils Stevenson, brother of photographer Ray Stevenson and eventually manager of Siouxsie And The Banshees.

How Nils came to be on the team I've never quite figured out but right from the start he became nothing more than Johnny Rotten's yes-man.

I assume he met Malcolm through Ray and bent Malcolm's ear for a job. I first met him at Dingwalls where Malcolm introduced us. He had hair down to his shoulders. Although he was alright I remember thinking, who is this long-haired git? Why do we need someone else?

Perhaps Malcolm had the idea that we would ultimately need a good road manager and we should take one on early by way of preparation. But Nils had no experience and you certainly don't need a road manager when you're going up to Whitley Bay for a gig at the local bingo hall – as we were at the time – and staying at a small bed and breakfast.

As far as I was concerned, there was no need for Nils. He just took up more room in the bloody Transit, which was cramped enough already, and became one more way for the lack of money to be split. It's not that I'm being tight with the money. It's that I could never understand Nils' role. I just thought of him as a leech who achieved something by association rather than effort.

He was someone who had no artistic input into the band whatsoever. His role was nothing more than being Malcolm's gopher and John's wet nurse. Yes John, no John, three bags full John. He licked up to both of them all the time.

He took over from John's entourage. He was more or less a one-man version of that entourage. Which meant John was hardly ever his own man.

John, however, did the best Kenneth Williams impersonation I've ever heard. He also seemed to enjoy carrying on his conversations in much the same manner as Kenneth Williams. One minute he'd be a paragon of eloquence and sophistication. The next he'd be full into his 'stop mucking about' persona with a whole heap of expletives thrown in for good measure.

He was also a very easy man to wind up. For example, there was the time he ended up storming off stage at The 100 Club. We'd always been working on cover versions in those days and one week we dug out an old Dave Dee, Dozy, Beaky, Mick And Tich song called 'He's A Raver'.

It was a stupid song, all about the clothes and the shoes the raver of the title was buying. We decided to pretend we were going to do it, just to wind John up. We knew he'd hate the idea of having to sing it.

So we studiously swotted it up and told him how great we thought it was. He kept on saying he wasn't sure if it was the right thing for us to do.

It so happened that our next show was the very first time we played The 100 Club. We had 'He's A Raver' all ready.

John must have been worried because he got really out of his box. Maybe he was worried about the size of the audience. There were his mates – Sid and Jah Wobble and John Grey – and some of the Bromley Contingent, and that was about it.

Although we'd convinced him we were going to do 'He's A Raver' he kept saying, I'm not doing it, I'm not doing it, I'll walk off stage. So, in the end we let him off the hook and agreed not to do it.

But he still had the hump and was really playing to all his mates, really showing off. He sang all the words to all the songs perfectly. The only trouble was that he sang all the words to a different song than the one we happened to be playing at the time. So, when we came to do 'Pretty Vacant' instead of singing the proper backing vocals, I started chanting at him, you're a cunt.

He got the hump even more over that – which I didn't blame him for because he was meant to. I was pissed off at him. Suddenly he looked at me and said, do you want a fight? Right there, on stage, in the middle of a show. Fuck off John, I said, we're supposed to be doing a gig.

At that he just snapped and ran straight off the stage, across the room and right up the stairs. He disappeared. The rest of us started vamping away the way people do when the singer's doing a costume change. Malcolm meanwhile went darting up the stairs after him.

A few minutes later the pair of them came back down the stairs into the club. John skulked across the room, came back on stage and glared at me. We attempted a couple more songs but it really wasn't working so we knocked it on the head. John shot straight off as soon as we left the stage.

Later I asked Malcolm what had happened. He told me that John had been outside in the street, standing at a bus stop waiting for a number 73 to take him home to Finsbury Park. Malcolm had told him that he had to go back on stage and apologise or be thrown out of the group.

John was back on stage like a shot when he said that because he realised Malcolm meant it. At that stage, John realised that being in the band meant he was onto a good thing. Let's be honest, there are never too many career openings for a 19-year-old Irish psychotic from North London.

The next time we rehearsed John was already there when I arrived. He was waiting for me, standing there with a four-pound hammer, swinging it in his hand. Call me a cunt, will you? he said.

We had a few words. I thought, I don't need this. And I walked out, turning my back on him. I figured that if he was going to do something, he'd do it then. So I was obviously watching over my shoulder ever so slightly. But he had no bottle to set about me. I just thought, what a wanker.

Yet all the arguing and threats were the strength of the band. Because when it came together it had such power. I've since read about The Who and their constant rows. Moon once turned up for a rehearsal with an axe intending to stave Daltrey's head in. But, unlike us, they stuck it out and kept on working together.

9

Paris, London... CHELMSFORD?

We'd made a name for ourselves that summer. The autumn was when we started to reach out beyond our small, hip following. We did TV shows, we played around the country, did interviews and started recording. Our first demos were done with Chris Spedding. As we'd known him from back in the early days of Malcolm's shop, I always assumed his wanting to come in and help us out was the action of a mate. I thought he came in to be our mentor purely out of the kindness of his heart. Subsequently, I found out that Mickie Most—who owned the RAK label, which Spedding was on—was interested in the band.

Malcolm made out that he was paying for those demos and that he would take the cost out of any gig money we made. In fact, Mickie Most paid for them. Spedding was his number one session guitarist at the time. And when he played his hit, 'Motorbikin', on *Top Of The Pops*, he and all his band were wearing clothes that they'd got from Malcolm's shop. The small world syndrome. And yet another illustration of Malcolm trying to pull a fast one on everyone else.

Years later, talking to Mickie Most, I found out what really happened. He and Malcolm had arranged to meet but Malcolm wouldn't meet him at his office because, he said, he didn't like his record company. So he insisted on meeting him at The Hilton Hotel. Straight off, Malcolm – who'd only talked to him on the phone before – proceeded to tell him that he didn't like his attitude. Then he told Mickie Most – one of the most successful record producers and record company owners of all time – exactly where he was going wrong. Malcolm had obviously set out to wind him up. Which he did. Mickie didn't want to know about us after that.

I've often wondered since what would have happened if we'd linked up with him. In retrospect, I think if we had signed to RAK it would have been a quite different game.

On the one hand, we wouldn't have had all the corporate shenanigans we had with EMI. On the other hand, we wouldn't have had the furor or the scandals that went with that. I suppose we'd have been more like one of Most's pop acts – Suzi Quatro, say – but with our own sound. At least we could have just got on with it.

An interesting idea, I think, because Mickie isn't the MOR pop person some people make him out to be. For example, a couple of years after that, he had a pop TV show called *Revolver*. Malcolm approached him with the idea of flying Ronnie Biggs into the country, landing him on the studio roof in a helicopter, filming him singing 'Cosh The Driver', then whisking him straight away again, before the authorities cottoned on. Right, said Mickie, you're on, Malcolm. But, strangely enough, he never heard from him again.

We did the demo session at Majestic Studios, a cinema converted into a 24-track studio just off Clapham High Road near the common.

I used Spedding's amp as my bass amp and that was the closest he came to playing with The Pistols while I was around. As always in the studio, things went slower than expected and the time went so quickly that we ran out of money before we got round to mixing what we'd recorded, which was three songs, 'Problems', 'No Feelings' and one other.

When I got home to Greenford – I'd had enough of the Denmark Street mice by then – my mum said, where have you been all day? I told her I'd been recording in the studio and suddenly she got all interested and asked to hear what I'd done.

So I played her the unmixed tape I'd brought home with me. Oooh, she said, I like the first one, it sounds just like The Shadows. That was 'Pretty Vacant'.

Our first TV appearance was on *So It Goes*, a show put together in Manchester, presented and produced by Tony Wilson. He was famous in Manchester even then, as the host of an early evening local news show. But he was also always involved in the music scene there: later he went on to set up Factory Records, New Order's label, and The Hacienda Club.

We'd already done a few gigs in Manchester, playing The Lesser Free Trade Hall twice that summer. The first time, right at the beginning of June, less than a hundred people turned up. But, although we didn't know it at the time, it was an incredibly influential gig. Morrissey was there, and so were Bernard Dicken, Peter Hook and Ian Curtis who went on to form Joy Division.

The second time we played it was towards the end of July. By that time Manchester had its own new bands. We were supported by Slaughter And The Dogs and The Buzzcocks – it was their very first gig.

I thought The Buzzcocks were wonderful. In fact I preferred them to The Clash at that stage because, whereas The Clash, it seemed to me, were trying to do the same as we were doing, only not as well, The Buzzcocks were doing something entirely different, with a totally different attitude. There was something funny about them. They were provincial and very sweet, although I'm sure they'd hate me saying that.

I was also really impressed by the way they managed to get themselves the support slot. They'd read a review of us in the *NME* and thought we sounded so great that they just had to see our next show. So they phoned the *NME* for details. The paper didn't have any but suggested they call Malcolm. So they came all the way down to London to the shop and found out about the next show. And they were so knocked out they immediately started their own band.

That night at The Lesser Free Trade Hall was also the first time we played 'Anarchy' in public. We packed it out and, because we'd booked it ourselves, we really made quite a bit of money. That's the night Tony Wilson saw us. Soon after, he invited us on to his late night TV show, which ran for a short while that summer.

We were on the show with Clive James – who wasn't nearly so well known back then. Originally they had just invited John, wanting him to do a solo interview. But John was a bit funny about it, not wanting to do things by himself. We decided we might as well insist that the whole band went on and that we played live. They agreed.

When we got there, their idea was that we'd just do the one number. But we don't want to do just the one number, we said, we want to do some warm-ups. We were just winding them up, to be honest.

However, they conceded. We're only going to film one number, they said, but you can do another as a warm-up, get the audience going a bit, then we'll record the second number, which would be 'Anarchy'.

We started into 'Problems'. Halfway through I broke a bass string. Blonk and it was gone. Nils, coming in useful for once, had to go and fetch another one. We had spare guitars and strings but in those days we didn't think to bring them on to the set with us.

The dressing room where we had left all the gear was about half a mile away. It took him about five minutes to get it, five minutes to bring it back, and five minutes to put it on. All the time the clock was tick-tocking away and everyone was going mad. This was Sunday night late and all the technicians were already on double time. If they overran it would turn into double double time.

Meantime, Tony Wilson took the floor to come the congenial host. He started to chat to Rotten. Well, tell me John, I asked you to come and do this interview by yourself but you turned it down. Are you too scared? Is it safety in numbers?

By this time I'd got the bass string on and was trying to get it in tune. For some reason I piped up, nah Tony, it's because you're a cunt. Totally in keeping with the punk rock spirit. Everyone laughed and as well as being red as a helmet he was absolutely stuck for words.

Why I said it, I'm not totally sure. It just seemed the right thing to do at the time, a bit of showmanship and a bit of a laugh. We'd had a bit of banter with him before the show, good-natured winding up, and it was a continuation of that. It wasn't meant nastily.

Sometimes our punk rock attitude was for real, sometimes it was put on a bit. In that particular instance, it was one hundred per cent assumed. It was like Iggy. On stage he's Iggy Pop but in private he's James Osterburg.

I think if you're going to portray some kind of corporate image you've got to back it up when it matters. Calling Tony Wilson a cunt was an example of that. On the other hand, though, it wasn't thought out in advance, it was totally spontaneous.

Snottiness had become a big part of being a Sex Pistol. We all got a taste for it as it became expected of us. You could always get a reaction with it. It also helped establish us in people's minds. When new bands come along they have to establish their ground and being snotty was a hell of a lot easier than just standing there saying, hello, it's us, anyone out there interested?

After I'd called Tony Wilson a cunt, Clive James got up and joined in. With his real gift of the gab he tried to pick an argument with John, a verbal fight practically. And John made mincemeat of him. He made Clive James look about this big. I was astonished. Clive James was doing all these TV shows at the time and was supposedly devastatingly articulate. Yet John had him on the ropes, simply by being so negative. Clive James didn't stand a chance. John kept saying, so what? And there's no answer to that.

A few mike stands went over at the end of 'Anarchy', nothing more. But all the technicians were rushing around so we high-tailed it back to our dressing room, where I suddenly remembered I'd left my bass on the stage.

When I got back to the studio it was deserted. The only person there was a little old bloke in a grey and maroon cardigan sweeping up. Here, he said, you in the band then? Yeah, I said, thinking I was about to get a right ticking off for foul language or one of the other things people were always on at us about.

Instead he said, I thought that was fucking smashing. It's about fucking time somebody shook those fucking cunts up. That was the best fucking thing I've ever seen on fucking TV. Well done, my lads.

One of the best known early pictures of us was taken at Heathrow Airport on our first trip abroad together. We're all sitting in a line on sofas looking glum. We were on our way to Paris to play at the opening night of a new club, The Chalet Du Lac.

The reason we were all so fed up was that Mr Management McLaren had forgotten his passport maybe by accident, maybe by design because he didn't want anyone seeing it. So we had to sit there waiting for this big furor to blow up and calm down. Finally it was agreed that Malcolm could travel without a passport. But it meant that we had to get a later flight.

On the plane we had champagne all round. It was Steve's birthday and my girlfriend Celia's 21st, and I was wondering if she'd got the 21 carnations I'd ordered to be delivered to her. Then John chipped in, we're going to crash, we're all going to die. I've never been the world's best flyer so I told him to shut up for fuck's sake which, thankfully, he did.

I was quite surprised by the number of people Malcolm knew in Paris. People like Michel Esteban who ended up being the E in Ze Records for a while but at the same time ran a shop called Harry Cover—it's a French pun, you pronounce it *haricot vert*.

Another of Malcolm's friends was Charles le Duc de Castelbarjac, a fashion designer who had a shop in the Place de la Marche de St Honore. He was extremely rich. He *lived* in The Hotel Brighton.

He was also very generous. He took us out on the town on the Friday night. As we didn't have to play till the following day—and then the Sunday—we could really live it up. He showed us how to drink tequila properly with the salt and the lemon, took us to Harry's Bar and Le Coupole one night and Le Dôme the next. Two good nights out on the slosh.

When we woke up on the Saturday morning Nils had disappeared with all our per diems—daily cash allowances—so none of us had any money for breakfast. While we were dying for a cup of coffee there was a phone call for Malcolm, from Dave Goodman.

What's up then boy? he said. You at the club?

No, the docks. They won't let us into the country. Something to do with a carnet.

We were all so green we didn't even know about needing a carnet to take your gear into a foreign country. It's a document which waives any excise duty on importing goods that you plan to take out again with you. Without one you're up there without a paddle.

They were able to sort out the carnet on the phone but it did mean the soundcheck was very late. We turned up at the club in the early evening. It was by a lake, obviously, out in the Bois de Vincennes, which is the Parisian equivalent of St John's Wood.

This was the day the club was meant to open and it was scarcely sorted out. There was a mad rush going down there. They were still painting things two hours before it opened—putting the chairs outside to dry—and making last minute alterations. Like laying the floor.

Despite the chaos there was a real atmosphere of expectation building up. We couldn't understand why. We were getting well paid, a grand I think, for two shows plus everything laid on. We thought it was great but we didn't really know the score as it turned out.

As time for the show approached it turned into pandemonium there. It was heaving inside. The club held maybe 2500 people. Outside another six or seven thousand had been trying to get in.

Our equipment van pulled up at about the same time as us. The crowd tried to turn the van over. The Bromley Contingent were there as well. They'd all decided to follow us over, turning it into a bit of a holiday, making the trip over squashed into an old yellow GPO van that Billy Idol was driving at the time.

Although we might have been a bit fed up with them in London, we were really pleased to see them in Paris – as you always are when you meet people you know from home when you're abroad. Siouxsie was being touched up left, right and centre – which was scarcely surprising as she was wearing suspenders, a peephole bra and sod all else.

The crowd was a real mish mash. As this was our first visit to Paris as a group we had no idea what to expect. We knew there wouldn't be too many punks. But we'd never have dreamed of what we did get.

There were 50-year-old blokes, the kind of people you'd find hanging around the Pigalle and construction worker types there with their grannies.

We thought, what the fuck? What the hell's going on? As we walked through I saw a woman in a gorgeous white dress sit down on one of those freshly painted chairs, then stand up and walk away with a black and white striped back to her gorgeous dress.

We played on a glass stage with lights beneath it. It was like something out of the science fiction movie *Soylent Green*. As I was jumping up and down a bloke at the corner of the stage kept on tugging my trouser leg and shouting, *le plafond, le plafond*. He obviously thought I was going to go through the stage.

They were like a football crowd out there. It was so packed

that one person clapping made the next person's arm move. A good show, but there was a funny atmosphere somehow. We still couldn't figure it out.

As it was Steve's birthday we went out and tied on a few. We were drinking in somewhere called Le Nashville. The state we were in we thought it was the height of hilarity that a flash bar in Paris should have the same name as a crummy pub rock venue back in Fulham.

Malcolm took us round by L'Odeon. All over the walls people had daubed the word 'Anarchie'. We thought, great, they know the words to our songs already. We didn't twig the truth – that it was all graffiti left over from 'les événements', the student uprising of 1968. And Malcolm didn't bother to put us right either.

The night finished off with Malcom and Steve going down the Rue St Denis. After a night of bending Malcolm's ear, Steve had finally convinced him that, it being his birthday, Malcolm should spring for a tart for him.

The second show at the Chalet du Lac was on the Sunday afternoon. We turned up to find the place no more than a third full. What's happening? we asked the promoter. Don't Parisians do anything on a Sunday afternoon? Is there a football match or something?

Oh no, he said, the first night here was *'entrée libre'*, but today, today they pay. Which explained why it had been so full the night before. Nothing is ever free in Paris. *Nothing*, that is, except The Sex Pistols' European debut.

Back in London Paul finally quit his job as an apprentice electrician and Malcolm started to take it really seriously, taking on Sophie Richmond as his P.A. She started working for him in his flat in Balham then moved on to his new offices in Dryden Chambers, right off Oxford Street.

W1 address, boy, he said when he got the offices, impressed by himself and hoping to impress me. Up till then he'd worked from home, surrounded by all the clobber from the shop.

The only thing about Dryden Chambers, though, was that someone had told me it was famous for being somewhere that *every* business that started out there went bankrupt there. (Which wasn't far off the mark as far as The Pistols were concerned but certainly wasn't true for Miles Copeland, who took an office downstairs and kept on trying to pinch ideas from Malcolm for this new band he'd put together called The Police.)

That long hot summer ended really with the last night we played The 100 Club, which was at the end of the summer. Ron Watts, who ran the place, had seen the punk movement build up over the summer and decided to put on a punk festival there.

The first night we played, supported by The Clash, Subway Sect and Siouxsie And The Banshees—who had Sid Vicious on drums. The Banshees were meant to have used The Clash's gear but when Bernie, their manager, saw Siouxsie wearing a swastika, he changed his mind. That Bernie, Sid announced from the stage, is a fucking little Jew.

The second night The Damned were the headlining band, with Stinky Toys—a French band—The Buzzcocks and The Vibrators also on the bill. That was the night when everything happened.

Sid chucked a glass, nearly blinding a girl. The Damned's drummer, Rat Scabies, started spitting at the audience. And they started spitting back. Thus was invented that grand tradition of gobbing. For a couple of years after that every time you played you'd come off stage covered in saliva, goobers hanging from your nose, thick wodges of phlegm on your top pocket.

And Sid invented the pogo. It was so crowded there was no room to dance. And he felt like a dance. So he started jumping up and down on the spot, like he was on a pogo stick, bashing into people all around him. As he was a big name on the punk scene other people started copying him.

One of the journalists there—Caroline Coon or John Ingham, most likely—spotted him and thought: yeah, we've got a movement going here, movements need a dance of their own, it looks like Sid's on a pogo stick, so let's call it after that. And so the pogo was born.

In a way that was the night punk really made the map. Sid Vicious as a star, gobbing, the pogo—they all started that night. And we weren't even there. We were off in Wales playing a gig.

It was at that very moment that Malcolm chose to present us with a management contract. Obviously we knew that he was working towards getting us a record contract. But that was about all we knew. We weren't privy to names or figures.

The fact that we were signing to EMI was pretty much sprung on us. Several record companies were chasing us but we didn't really know much about what was going on because we were doing a lot of gigs. Malcolm came to very few of them and he certainly didn't go out of his way to tell us about his negotiations.

The first we saw of this was the management contract, which Malcolm produced after a gig one night, telling us it had been drawn up by Steven Fisher, his lawyer and a remarkably oily character. That was when I—and the rest of the band—realised that something was most definitely up.

I was the only one who read the contract. Paul might have looked at it but the rest just didn't bother. And what Malcolm was asking seemed ridiculous. He wanted to take 25 per cent plus we were to cover all his expenses.

I saw it as a proper contract, one which you should get into a bit of negotiation over. So I tried to knock him down. But the others didn't back me up at all. Steve's attitude was simple. If Malcolm stitched us up, he'd break his fucking legs. Paul was sympathetic to me, knowing I was right, but as usual not wanting to cause a stir. And John, Mr Cleverclogs, didn't even read the contract. He signed it then turned round to me and said, if there's anything wrong with this it's *your* fault because *you've* read it.

If they'd all stuck by me we could have knocked him down a bit. It wasn't an outrageous contract but it was a bit over the top. I tried to start bargaining from 10 per cent. I must have heard that figure somewhere, the idea of managers being 'Mr 10 Per Cents'. Yet we ended up paying 25 – which is the norm for contracts today but only because mugs like us set the precedent. And so much for Steve breaking Malcolm's legs. Last time I saw Malcolm he wasn't even limping.

When we did sign to EMI there was a good bit of money around at last. Ah, I thought, I could really do with some new gear and here's my chance.

I got a new guitar straight away but I still wasn't happy with my amp and speaker cabinet. It was a little four by 12 job with the speakers angled inward. Perfect for a small club but once we started playing on larger stages it was just no good, it didn't punch the sound out, you could hardly hear it. So I was after getting a new amp.

My chance came up at a gig we played specially for TV. London Weekend Television had called Malcolm up and asked if we'd do a programme on punk rock to be presented by Janet Street Porter. When we agreed, it was arranged that the show would be built around a gig we were doing at the Notre Dame Hall, just off Leicester Square.

But first we did an interview with her in our Denmark Street place. And, to be honest, I think she must have had the hots for John because the rest of us scarcely got a look in. It was the Janet and John show.

But none of us were worried because we didn't take the programme at all seriously. It went out during the day on a Sunday so we thought that it was just another ethnic minority show, something that no one who was hip enough to be interested in would be up in time to see. Later, I learned that we were wrong, that loads of Pistols fans first saw us on that show.

At the gig itself I remember how pissed off I was with my amp and how I wanted an Acoustic stack. Right, I thought, I can kill two birds with one stone here. One, I can look really wild. Two, I get new gear out of it.

So, right at the end of the set, I stuffed the neck of my bass right into the front of the hated cabinet. Whump, that put paid to that and made sure Malcolm would shell out for a new Acoustic set-up. Unfortunately, though, we got called back for an encore. So there I had to stand like a lemon, miming all the way through 'Submission'.

10

Strike!

now it was time to make our first record. There was some debate about which song it should be but not much. I must admit I pushed hard for 'Pretty Vacant' – not just because I wrote it but also because it was our most developed song. For a long time it had been our standard bearer, the song which summed us up most completely.

But then 'Anarchy In The UK' came along. And that really was *the* statement. We'd premiered it at that gig in Manchester earlier in the year and it had enormous impact right from the start. We took to opening our set with it. So, when the time came for a discussion on what should be the first single, 'Anarchy' won hands down.

Although the Spedding demos had come to very little, we'd also done some recording with Dave Goodman. He produced the demos which impressed EMI enough to sign us so we thought, fine, let's use him to produce 'Anarchy'.

Malcolm wanted Dave to do it and Dave wanted Dave to do it. We thought: give it a shot.

First we went into Lansdowne Studios. It was our first time in a big studio but we weren't intimidated by it that much. We thought they were lucky to have us there – although they didn't quite agree.

But that's the attitude we adopted and it's a good one. If you're trying to record something while you're feeling intimidated by the technology, it's not going to come out right on the tape.

We had a week in there and it still didn't sound right by the end of the week. We played it again and again and again, pretty well most of the time, we thought.

But nobody could make up their mind. There was no shortage of bodies around to venture an opinion. Malcolm was there a lot of the time. So were Ray Stevenson and Dave's partner Kim Thraves. Loads of people, but no one who knew enough about music to know what was great and who had the bottle to say, that's it, that's the one, we can all pack up.

We moved on to Wessex Studios. We were getting remarkably cheesed off. The song wasn't sounding any better. In fact it must have been getting worse. Dave was casting around for things to alter. He – and Malcolm – started trying to get us to play faster and that was a disaster. As I've said before, this ran counter to what we considered The Pistols' sound to be about. The Pistols always sounded best when they were playing at a steady, confident pace, not too fast.

There must have been lots of times during that week when we did play it exactly right but still no one had the guts to say, yeah, that's the one.

We were wasting a fortune in recording time. Plus Dave was using up reel after reel of two-inch tape, at God knows what a reel. On some of the reels were the other songs we'd knock out when we got bored – the great version of 'No Fun', for example, which eventually surfaced on the B-side of 'God Save The Queen'. But most of the tape was just stuffed with attempts at 'Anarchy'.

Why don't you go back over them? I asked Dave. Nah, he said, I'll keep it for my home studio. At God knows what a reel, paid for out of our advance.

John was really getting frustrated. He'd turn up in the evening and give us a hard time. Haven't you done it yet?

You're fucking useless, you lot. The papers are right, you can't even play. I never thought I'd believe the *Sun*.

In the end Steve, Paul and I went on strike. Look, we said, we've played it really well loads of times but it's still not good enough, it's not working out. We didn't turn up at the studio for a couple of days.

Paul meanwhile came up with the idea of using Chris Thomas as a producer. I wasn't that familiar with his work but Paul was really into Roxy Music, who Chris had produced. He played a few of their albums to Malcolm.

Now, I'm sure Malcolm couldn't tell what he was meant to be listening for – production is such an intangible thing, how can you sort out who's responsible for what? What's the band's contribution? How much is down to the song? What does the producer actually put into that stew?

I've always thought a producer's job is to be the person who has to sprinkle ooffle dust over it all just to make sure it goes alright. Whatever Malcolm thought about all this, he said, OK, let's try Chris Thomas.

We – minus John, who hadn't deigned to come – went round to Chris Thomas's house in Ealing. His wife, an absolutely gorgeous Japanese woman, was there as well. We already knew her as she was one of the Sadista Mika Band and was always coming into Malcolm's shop when it was Let It Rock.

He seemed pretty interested in working with us. He'd heard what we'd done and liked the song. Great chord changes, he said, who wrote them?

I had, of course. When he said that it seemed to really piss off Steve and Paul. Personally speaking, I felt I could live with the compliment.

A couple of days later we were in the studio with him. We moved that fast because there was already a release date scheduled for 'Anarchy' and no one wanted to lose the momentum of all the press we'd generated.

Again we were in Wessex. I think it's *the* rock 'n' roll studio, really. The day we arrived we opened the door to the wrong studio by mistake. There was Freddie Mercury going at it at full operatic pelt. He looked at us like we were something the cat had dragged in. We'd walked in on the middle of the take but, as they'd forgotten to switch on the red 'Recording In Progress' light, they could hardly blame us.

We spent a morning setting up, making sure the sound was right. Bill Price, Wessex's engineer, did that, thinking of tiny little things which would improve the sound.

For instance, he picked up a metal flight case and set it at an angle by Steve's Twin Reverb amp to give a better reflection of the sound, producing a slightly harder edge. This was a real attention to detail which we'd not had before.

He also set up a couple of ambient mikes, to record all the peripheral sounds in the room. When you mix that in with all the other music it gives you a bigger, more immediate and 'liver' sound. It makes the tracks sparkle.

And so we started playing, running straight through five takes. That took us up to about four in the afternoon. Chris said, oh, I think we've got it there, let me just try this.

He took the first half of one take and the second half of another and spliced them together, then played us the result. It worked.

The only thing wrong was a slight timing discrepancy on the snare drum during one of the verses. They got round that by rigging up a tape delay to double the snare pattern. That made a blemish into a feature. And, hey presto, we had one cracking rhythm track. All we needed was John to add the vocals. Where was John?

He rolled up about seven. I suppose you lot haven't fucking done it yet, he said. Punk rock, that's you all over. You're useless, you lot, you can't play.

OK then, clever clogs, we said, you just get in there and sing. We've done it. What do you mean you've done it? We've done it. Just like we've been saying all along, we've been playing it well enough. All it needed was somebody to realise when it was good enough. Now it sounds great.

John did his vocals and, after a couple of days' break, we

went back in to do some overdubs – extra guitar from Steve, basically.

But I started sticking my oar in. I'm the guitarist, Steve said, why don't you sling your hook down the pub and let me do it? Which was fair enough. I opened the door to go and guess who was at the door, bent double? Freddie Mercury. Oh, he said, do you know where the toilets are?

You've been in here a month already, Freddie, and you don't know where the toilets are?

Yeah, right, right, he said, OK, OK.

Of course he'd been earwigging at the door trying to find out what all this punk rock was about. He'd heard that we were out to destroy dinosaur bands like his and he was checking out his would-be assassins.

When I came back from the pub Steve had finished his overdubs. Then Chris Thomas mixed it with Bill and it was all finished.

I don't know what the other guys did but when you get your first record you think, this is going to be great. Then you put it on and whatever you hear it's an assault on your eardrums. It's like hearing your voice recorded for the first time.

When I played it I hated 'Anarchy' so much that I turned the record into an ashtray – and I didn't even smoke then. But a couple of days later I heard it again and thought, hang on, it's not so bad after all, in fact, it's really rather good.

11

The
'Filth'
And The
Fury

If there's one thing everyone—even it they've never listened to rock 'n' roll record in their life—knows about The Sex Pistols, it's that we appeared on the Bill Grundy show, we swore and some bloke got so annoyed by us he kicked in his TV set.

It was December 1 and we were rehearsing for the 'Anarchy' tour in the usual kind of dump you use to rehearse in. This particular dump was in Harlesden, right around the corner from where I grew up.

It used to be a cinema. I went there to see an X-rated movie—*I Am Curious, Yellow*—the very first day I was old enough to see one legitimately. I'd seen them before, of course, but that's not the same thing. That's the thrill of sneaking in. When you're old enough, that's the thrill of being grown up.

I tried to pay but the bloke on the door said, you're under-age, I'm not letting you in. I had to go home and fetch my birth certificate and come back. By the time I'd waited for two buses and got back to the cinema he'd gone home for the day and I'd missed half the film. I felt a right twerp.

We were using this cinema for full stage rehearsals. It was a package tour—us, The Clash, The Heartbreakers and The

Damned – and we had to practise equipment changeovers and time each band's set.

It was all a bit confusing. Apart from us, by far the best-known band of the other three were The Damned. But the consensus was that they shouldn't be second on the bill – which is how they were advertised – but bottom.

Rat Scabies will always say that the main reason they were on the tour was nothing to do with punk solidarity or any ideas of Larry Parnes-style package tours. He says they were on it because Malcolm had realised that they'd already played loads of shows around the country and had proved to be good crowd pullers.

So Malcolm got them on the tour, despite the fact that he couldn't stand their manager, Jake Riviera. They meant more bums on more seats, nothing more. Well maybe also the fact that they paid their own way – i.e., we didn't have to pick up the tab for their travelling expenses.

We turned up at Harlesden about halfway through The Heartbreakers' set. This was the band formed by Malcolm's old mates from New York, Johnny Thunders – who was in The New York Dolls – and Richard Hell, who I've already mentioned. Hell had since departed and it was now down to a four-piece featuring Thunders, Walter Lure, Jerry Nolan – also from The Dolls – on drums and Billy Rath on bass. They sounded really good and, like most American bands, could really play. We'd seen all these new English punk bands who sounded so weak. But The Heartbreakers were really cock-sure and confident, most likely because of all the gigs they'd done between them.

I got talking to Mick Jones. There's a really weird rumour going round, he said. Walter Lure – The Heartbreakers' other singer and guitarist and a perfect foil to Johnny Thunders – has a brain tumor and only has weeks to live. So we were all pleasant to Walter.

None of it was true. He just looked a bit pale. Never seeing daylight, you would. And those glasses always made him look a bit spazzy. These days he works on Wall Street and makes a fortune, or so Thunders would have it.

Although Malcolm used to manage The Dolls we'd never met any of them. When they'd finished playing we went over and introduced ourselves.

Jerry Nolan, the drummer, sat down next to me. I really enjoyed the band, I said, I really liked that one called 'Chinese Rocks'. Oh yeah, he said, I really like that one myself – pleased he was, but cocky like he is. What's it about then, that one? I asked. He looked right at me as if I had the brain of a tablecloth and said in that big, booming American voice of his, he-ro-in, boy.

Nice, I said, lovely. But I still didn't think any more about it. I was very innocent about hard drugs in those days.

We were just sitting around waiting to go on for our set run through. Nils came over and said, there's a big, black limousine outside waiting for you, a Daimler. It's to take you to do some TV show.

We're not going, we all said. We've got rehearsing to do, and we don't like that car. Nils got on the phone to Malcolm, then came back and told us what Malcolm had said: do it, boys, or you won't get your wages this week. Twenty-five pounds a week is no one's fortune but it's certainly better than trying to survive on nothing.

There was some more to-ing and fro-ing on the phone, Malcolm telling us this, us demanding that. But finally and inevitably we all climbed into this big, black – and very comfortable – Daimler. We drove off into the North London winter damp with no idea of where we were going. All we knew was that we were doing a TV show. Malcolm hadn't bothered to tell us which one.

EMI were putting the push in for us. 'Anarchy' had just come out, the 'Anarchy' tour started in two days' time and the EMI corporate machinery had begun to roll, like some lugubrious steamroller. At this time EMI was still a power in the land, coasting on its Beatles years. With their clout they'd been able to get us on *Today* – a pretty good stroke for a new band with their first record only just out. A live show, *Today* ran straight after the national news.

When we bowled up to the studio – at Thames TV, beneath Euston Tower in Marylebone Road – Malcolm was there to meet us. In the lobby everyone gave us funny looks but we just thought, fuck 'em.

We were ushered straight into the green room as if they wanted to hide us away as fast as they could. An attendant in a liveried jacket asked us, would you like a drink, young fellers? We all thought we'd get something stronger but all he offered us was soft drinks or beer. We made do with half a can of warm lager apiece.

Then the attendant left the room and we went straight for the drinks cupboard and got stuck in. We had a lot more than we were supposed to but it was still only a few cans of beer. Nobody was drunk. But we were all a bit loosened up.

We wandered through into the studio and standing there were the Bromley Contingent. Siouxsie's tits were more or less hanging out – again. I thought, oh no, we want to do our stuff as a group and there's these bleeding Herberts again.

Malcolm was still going on with his idea to make it look like some big Movement, with a capital M. We'd already done *Young Nationwide* with the Bromley Contingent. Once was OK. But I had got a bit fed up with them hanging about all the time.

As it was a live programme we had to wait around in the studio while they did the frst bit of the show. It's always boring waiting. We all started chatting. I might have been fed up that Siouxsie was there but it was nothing personal, I still talked to her. Someone passed a drink around. There was a bit of a free-for-all, pushing and shoving and joshing.

Next thing the cameras were on us and Bill Grundy seemed like he'd got some kind of cob on. The rest is history, really.

He started asking us questions in turn, starting with me. He waved a pile of papers around, looked into the camera and said, I'm told *that* group have received £40,000 from a record

John, Steve, Glen and Paul on the roof of Malcolm's office at Dryden Chambers, Oxford Street, London. (Barry Plummer)

The Pistols at the 100 Club, London. (Rex Features)

Glen and Steve at The Nashville in London.
(Glen Matlock collection)

The Pistols at the Chalet du Lac, Paris, 1976.
(Glen Matlock collection)

Glen and Steve, Paris, 1976. (Rex Features)

John, Glen, Steve and Paul. (Rex Features)

Two shots from a photo session on Denmark Street,
October 6, 1976. (Bob Gruen)

Glen and Sid Vicious, The Vicious White Kids show at the Electric Ballroom, Camden Town, London. (Rex Features)

The Pistols on the Serpentine lake in London's Hyde Park. (Rex Features)

company. Doesn't that seem to be slightly opposed to their anti-materialistic view of life?

It was a stupid question, presumably meant in a lightweight and inconsequential way. So I gave him a lightweight and inconsequential answer. No, I said, the more the merrier.

There were a few more like that. Silly questions and silly answers with us treating it as a laugh. He started talking about Beethoven, Mozart and Bach. Why, I don't know. But I just joked back. They're all heroes of ours, ain't they, I said.

There was a bit more banter then John said shit, very quietly and by mistake. He covered up really well. But Grundy kept pressing him, asking him what he'd said. What was the rude word? So John said it aloud. Shit.

Was it really? said Grundy. Good heavens, you frighten me to death. Then he turned to the girls—Siouxsie and the others—and tried to drag them into the conversation.

When he asked Siouxsie if she'd meet him afterwards, Steve went into Warp Factor Five and weighed right into him. You dirty old sod, you dirty old man.

Grundy just wound him up. Keep going chief, you've got another five seconds. Say something outrageous. So Steve told him he was a dirty fucker, a fucking rotter. (Rotter? That one cracked me up.) Grundy turned to the camera. Well that's it for tonight. I'll be seeing you soon. I hope I'm not seeing you again. (That was to us.) From me, though, goodnight. And that was it.

All the time I could see Malcolm behind the cameras. He had his head in his hands. I couldn't hear him but he looked like he was laughing. Not because he thought it was funny but out of nerves. He was shitting himself.

His attitude was, oh no, you've gone and done it now, what the hell are we going to do? A long way from the idea a lot of people had that it was all his scheme. There was no little Malcolm the machiavellian telling us to go and swear our heads off on TV so we could scoop all the publicity.

The oddest thing at the time, though, was that none of us

could work out what Grundy was up to. Why did he keep pushing John and Steve to swear?

Years later I got an answer of sorts. I met a journalist in my local. He'd known Grundy through work – or the Fleet Street grapevine. His version of that evening was that Grundy hadn't wanted to interview us. It wasn't because he thought the show shouldn't do anything on punk but that he didn't know enough about it himself and felt someone else should do the interview. Or perhaps he just didn't think we were worth giving the time of day to. After all, he was the very first man to interview The Beatles on TV, for Granada in the early sixties. He must have considered us well beneath him.

It turned into a control room power struggle. He felt that if he didn't want to do something he shouldn't have to do it. His idea was that he should have last call on what was on the show.

His producer saw it differently. He laid it down to Grundy the way it was. Which was: do it or get out, I call the shots here. There was a face-off in the control room and Grundy lost.

By the time he went on the air he'd already had enough of it. So he vented his frustration on us. Frankly, he couldn't give a damn about anything at that point. Plus he'd obviously had a few.

Funnily enough, I did see him one more time. It was about six months after I left The Pistols. I had a 1956 Sunbeam Talbot then, a big, beaten up, battle-bus of a motor. I was getting The Rich Kids together then and Steve New and Rusty Egan were with me in the car. We happened to drive past the Thames TV studios. And Bill Grundy came out of the building. It was the middle of the day but to me it looked like he'd just cleared his desk out, ready to leave for good. He had a briefcase in each hand and bundles of papers under each arm.

The car stopped at the lights and we gave him a right ribbing. Oi, Bill, remember me? He stared at me and obviously did. By the way he looked at Steve and Rusty he must have thought they were Pistols too. And probably, as far as he was concerned, The Pistols were the people who had sent his whole career down the poop chute.

He stood there on the kerb eyeballing us. Then he carefully put down his briefcases and papers and looked to the left, looked to the right, looked behind him. Then he just went, wallop, giving us two fingers with each hand. At last he'd been able to tell The Pistols to fuck off. And he was having a great time doing it, really enjoying himself.

The lights changed and I drove off. That was the last I saw of Bill Grundy. In fact, it was probably the last anyone saw of Bill Grundy.

Straight after the show, we walked out through the studio, still having a bit of a laugh about it all. I wanted to get back in the green room for another drink.

But Malcolm was having none of it. He literally dragged me out of the building and shoved me into the motor with the rest of them. We glided away up Euston Road.

As we did a police car turned up – just as well I didn't stop for another drink – and half a dozen coppers piled out and into Thames TV, obviously looking for us and some action. We gave them the finger out of the back window.

Malcolm was really worried. Oh God, I think we've gone and done it now. I don't know what's going to happen. So much for any kind of prepared McLaren master plan.

When we got back to Harlesden to finish up the rehearsal the others asked us how it had gone. Don't worry, we told them, you'll find out soon enough.

I went home to my flat in Chiswick, where I'd moved as soon as possible after we'd signed to EMI. Straightaway my dad was on the phone. In those days I used to call my folks and tell them every time I was going to be on TV. I'm sure all the guys in the band did, except maybe Steve.

Glen, Glen, my dad was saying, what have you gone and done now? Bit like Malcolm, really. I don't mind you doing what you have to do to get on in this world, even if it does mean swearing on TV. Fair enough. But we'd rung up the whole family so they could all watch it as well. There was your Uncle Colin and your cousin Sarah. She was watching and she's only eight. Your mum's very upset.

Here's me, I thought, trying to do something special and that's all my dad can say, that your cousin Sarah's eight years old and she's heard you swear – as if she'd never heard a swear word before in her life.

A couple of days later John's mum was in the papers or on TV really sticking up for him, saying I don't bloody well care if my son swore on TV, it's about time somebody shook things up a bit. And swearing her head off all the time.

I was impressed. I thought, why can't my parents stick up for me like that? There's my dad, a good union man all his life, not being able to see that we were trying to carry a torch for the common man – not with our swearing on TV or our music, perhaps, but certainly with our confrontational behaviour.

I didn't speak to my mum for about a week. When I finally did talk to her all she could say was, Glen, it's terrible what you've done, you used to be such a nice boy, now every time I go to work at the gas board they call me Mrs Sex Pistol.

I had to stop myself laughing at that. But I also wondered why she couldn't see what we were trying to do. And what harm could a little bit of swearing on TV do to anyone? Walk down any street and you'll hear some building labourer swearing his head off.

And what about the bloke who was so disgusted by us that he kicked his TV set in?

Berk.

The next morning Sophie from Malcolm's office called and woke me up. There's a meeting at EMI, she said, can't explain now, just get there *tout de suite*. So, dutifully, I scrubbed my teeth and washed my balls and walked to the bus stop.

Standing there already was a girl I'd seen around the area for a while and who I really fancied. Blonde and pert, she looked like one of those 'ravers' in *Carry On* movies, those girls who never did much except run around shrieking in their underwear.

Maybe she was an actress. I think I saw her on *Doctor Who*. And she'd been making eyes at me for a couple of weeks.

Or so I thought. Maybe she just thought I was dressed a bit outlandishly.

Of course, although the story about us was all over the front pages that morning, I hadn't seen any of them. And I hadn't seen the show itself because it went out live and no one had videos in those days. So I had no idea of the fuss that was going on.

But as soon as I saw this girl's face at the bus stop I knew exactly how much fuss was going on. The dirty look she gave me, it was like I'd just crawled out of a swamp and was coming to get her. Ah ha, I thought, the Bill Grundy show.

I got off the bus at Marble Arch and walked round to Manchester Square. The other three guys were already there, hanging out of an upstairs window. John Blake and the rest of the Fleet Street pop pack were milling around.

It was a big press conference. Whether it was Malcolm's idea or EMI twisted his arm I just don't know. But in one way it was certainly an eye-opener for me. For the first time I got first-hand experience of the British gutter press.

One particular photographer said he wanted to take a group picture of us all together and handed us a couple of cans of beer each. We were all sitting in a line. Can you sit a bit closer? asked the photographer. Steve said: I'm not getting any closer to him–meaning John–he's got smelly armpits.

Partly he was acting up for the press but he was also deliberately winding John up. There was always a bit of good-natured bantering going on between them. Steve and Paul were always taking the piss out of John while still letting him carry on behaving the way he did.

(By the way, Paul's public persona can best be summed up by the way he behaved on the Grundy show. While Steve danced and swore his head off, Paul's only contribution was to feign a yawn. That's Paul all over.)

With me it was different, and that was always my problem with the group. When I had a ruck with John I would really mean it. Steve and Paul got as fed up with him as I did but they'd never do anything more about it than take the piss.

Meanwhile back at the press conference, I was drinking my beer. I burped and, like any well brought up lad, said sorry, pardon me. The next day in the papers this appeared as: they wouldn't move closer together on account of Johnny Rotten's stinking armpits and, when the bass player was asked a question, he just belched.

I thought, hang on, I said pardon but they didn't bother to print that bit. It's a cliche but it's true—until you've been roughed up by the tabloids you can't quite believe how it happens. They just use you as they see fit to sell their papers.

The other surprise for me that day was Malcolm. He had totally changed overnight. The previous evening in the car he'd been really worried about what might happen. Now, the following morning, he saw how he might turn it all to our—and his—advantage.

His greatest strength was never that he was a great manipulator. He wasn't some Svengali with a giant master plan in his head. He was an opportunist—something he might have learned through his years attached to the Situationists.

He was brilliant at making the best of an opportunity. And the Bill Grundy show was one god-sent to set the ball rolling. Instead of having to create press interest, it was all there ready to tap. Which is a wonderful position for any manager to be in.

The group took it all quite lightly. We didn't think, wasn't it great that we swore on TV last night? We just thought how stupid it was that we'd let slip a couple of swear words when it was *Grundy* who kept encouraging us to swear—and there was now this enormous hoo hah.

But Malcolm, Malcolm saw it differently. He knew how he could exploit it to his best advantage. All he had to do was rise to the occasion. And he certainly did that.

12

Once
AROUND
The Block

the 'Anarchy' tour started out from our Tin Pan Alley base. Malcolm turned up with a whole load of new clothes from his shop for us and we all piled into the bus that was parked outside Denmark Street. We had no idea of what was about to happen. As far as we knew, we'd been booked into a series of halls and we were going to play gigs in them, promote the single, rock out and generally have a good time. And that was it. We had no idea of the fuss that would blow up or how the entire tour would collapse around us.

At that time, with all the other bands touring with us, it looked like it could be a lot of fun. The Clash we already knew. And The Heartbreakers, well, no one would call them a nice bunch of guys but they seemed OK by us. The Damned, though, didn't travel with us. At first we didn't understand why but as the tour went on – well, staggered on – we gradually began to understand. Malcolm and The Damned's manager, Jake Riviera, had locked horns.

Jake came from a pub rock background and had no time for Malcolm, who he saw as little more than a jumped-up shmutter merchant, with no understanding of the music or the business. Malcolm thought of Jake as a real pleb. The Bill Brown of rock 'n' roll he called him, nothing but darts, public bars and pints of bitter.

They hated each other and did everything they could to do the other one down. Yet, like it or not, these two enemies had ended up managing the number one and number two punk bands in the country. So they agreed to work together on the tour. As things turned out it was the uneasiest of truces.

When we set off from Denmark Street, all that was far from our minds and away into the future. Driving off we felt like the cat's whiskers in our brand new togs. (Of course, much later we discovered that Malcolm charged us – a lot – for all these clothes from *his* shop. And I never got a bloody tax deduction for them, because of his slapdash accounting.)

All three bands were in the coach together. And after the first gig that coach was followed everywhere by a parade of press vehicles. As we'd check out of a hotel so would they. Down the motorway we'd go. Down the motorway they'd go, arriving at the next hotel just after us.

The major memory of the tour is boredom. We spent most of our time hanging around hotels, just waiting. As gig after gig was canceled, we had no idea of what would happen next – or what was happening at the time. We'd just sit around hoping they could find somewhere we would be allowed to play. That's probably why the whole tour is a bit of a blur in my mind.

It comes back as a series of almost unconnected incidents. Like throwing potted plants around in the lobby of The Dragonara Hotel, Leeds. The newspaper reporters had asked us to do it and, winding them up, we said we would if they paid for the damage. To our surprise they said they would.

The hotel manager, who was a young bloke, really enjoyed it. As the reporters were paying he didn't care a fig about us slinging the plants around. He just thought it was funny.

So when the papers called up later, asking about this 'outrage', he said he didn't mind at all, the damage had been paid for. Which left the papers without a story and feeling quite deflated. It was splendid seeing the *Sun* being given the cold shoulder.

I learned a lot about the tabloid press on that tour. Once we had to run a gauntlet of reporters to get onto the coach. As I pushed through I could hear them saying, they're going to speak to us, they're going to speak to us. I didn't say a dickie bird.

One of the first on the coach, I took a seat about halfway to the back. John got on after me. The windows were open and I could hear a couple of journalists talking in the car park.

Did you speak to him? said one of them, meaning John. No, said the other, got nothing out of him. I did, said the first one, happy as a bird and really proud of himself. I got two 'shits' and a 'fuck' out of him.

As the tour went on the whole party broke up into factions. Mick Jones was my mate. We hung out together, roomed together and had a laugh together on the coach.

We'd also eat together most evenings – when we had the money. Mick had just turned vegetarian about two weeks previously and this caused problems. One night in Leeds we went for a meal at an Italian restaurant.

As there was nothing on the menu that Mick could eat, not even an omelette, he agreed to have a trout. When the waiter brought it, it still had its head on. Mick nearly threw up on the spot. What's a matter? said the waiter in a thick Leeds Italian accent, genuinely having no idea of what was wrong.

Can't you take it away and cut the head off, I said. Which he did, only when he brought it back all he'd done was lop off the head, move it half an inch from the body and shove a piece of lettuce between the two. Mick wouldn't even look at it. He walked straight out.

Christ, I thought, these people up North really are a bit thick. This was the first time we'd spent much time up there and I was struck by the cultural divide. It wasn't so much a case of thinking the government wasn't giving a fair share of the money to the North as reckoning God hadn't given them a fair share of brain cells.

Malcolm did a famous interview for TV when we were in Leeds. He was asked something like, people say you're sick, well, are you?

Malcolm jumped right back at them. Sick? Certainly we're sick. We're sick of what's going on in this country. We're sick of people's attitudes. We're sick of this government.

I thought that was really clever, not denying anything but turning it right around on the interviewer. Offence as defence.

Our first night in the city we all decided to go out and try to pick up girls, a Monday night it was. Right from the beginning of the tour we'd had a security guy with us. A really fat bloke, he'd been on the road with bands for years and knew everything there was to know about touring, whereas we knew just about nothing.

He said he didn't fancy going out, he'd rather stay in the hotel. As soon as we'd gone he pulled the best looking receptionist in the hotel and had her in the bath. He had sussed that on the road you make do with what's around rather than going out looking in Leeds on a Monday night. He knew that and we didn't.

On the other hand he did get stuck in the bath. Someone had to help him and the receptionist out. *And* he had a rotten cold for the rest of the tour.

My main memory of the show at Cleethorpes Winter Gardens is a pair of boots that Malcolm had sold me. Almost like biker boots, with quite high heels, they were supposed to be really well made. But one of the heels fell off, leaving half a dozen three-inch nails sticking out – no joke when the heels are that high. When I walked around I looked like John Cleese doing the Ministry of Funny Walks.

Malcolm, I said, give me some money to get my shoes fixed. I can't go on hobbling around like this.

What are you on about boy? he said. You're supposed to be a punk rocker. What's a missing heel to you?

Malcolm, I want some fucking money.

He gave it to me, finally. But he obviously had the hump as well about me pestering him. He already had enough on his mind without the bass player tapping him for a couple of quid. But I couldn't walk until the heel was fixed so that was all I could think about.

In Caerphilly the hall was surrounded by religious maniacs trying to stop people getting in. It was also one of the first times I ran across Steve Strange, who later became our roadie in The Rich Kids and then famous as a club owner and founder of the whole New Romantics scene – along with Rich Kids drummer Rusty Egan.

The *NME* jazz critic, Brian Case, came down to Caerphilly to write about it. Not for the *NME*, who weren't interested – they thought we were a passing phase – but for *The Observer Magazine*, who put his story on the front cover.

It was a wonderful article – great rows going on outside among the local politicians, all obviously only interested in making whatever political capital they could make out of the situation and doing whatever they could to increase their votes at the next election. For the first time in ages we read something about ourselves where the writer had actually put some thought into what he was writing. After weeks of the *Sun* and the *Daily Mirror* chasing us around it was a real relief.

In Manchester, I remember, we played at The Electric Circus, where someone threw a bottle of brown ale at me on stage. It could easily have killed me. And on the coach there, Strummer, in his paint-splattered Jackson Pollock clothes, an idea pinched from yours truly, started a big ruck about not wanting a particular journalist to be on there with us.

Fucking Ada, Joe, someone – maybe me – said, you're only the first band on the bill, you know. That shut him up.

It wasn't him coming on with a punk rock attitude. It was him coming on like a pop star, getting delusions of grandeur and ideas above his station. The journalist had probably written something he wasn't too happy about – the fact that he went to a public school, maybe.

At that stage The Clash had no clout. As I said, they looked like a bunch of squatters, everything was done – out of necessity mind you – so cheaply. If Strummer had looked like Rotten then what he said would have carried some weight. But he didn't, he looked like what he was, someone who'd just left the 101ers.

Malcolm spent most of his time in London, dealing with all the shit going down at EMI, but on one of his visits he started really bending my ear about The Damned, trying to get them slung off the tour. We were backstage at Leeds Poly, talking while they were playing.

What do you think of them then? he asked, deliberately playing the devil's advocate. They're alright, I said, I'm not particularly knocked out one way or the other. But he went on. Don't you think they spoil it? The Clash and The Heartbreakers are great, but The Damned are awful, they're bringing it all down.

Later I realised this was all part of his face-off with Jake Riviera, trying to stir trouble because he wanted to lob them off the tour and find a crafty way to do it. I think it also had something to do with the money.

With one band less on the package, the money would be split three rather than four ways. Although we hadn't been supporting The Damned financially, they did get their split of the door money and so perhaps Malcolm was trying to claw a little of that back for the rest of us.

One night I went to have a drink with The Damned and ended up on their tour bus, going back to their hotel with them. While we were staying in expensive five star places, they were in some bed and breakfast. Wouldn't you rather be with us? I said.

We would, we would, they said to a man.

On the other hand, I remember thinking they seemed to be getting more of a real taste of life on the road than we were. At least they were free agents and could travel around where they wanted. They weren't holed up in hotels for days on end like us, not knowing what the fuck was going on.

But in the end they put the nails in their own coffin by agreeing to play in front of Derby Borough Council Leisure

Committee. The idea was that if the Committee thought we were OK then we could play in the city. If they didn't we couldn't. Nothing but narrow-minded, pig ignorant, provincial censorship. So we refused to do it, but The Damned didn't. That was it, they were off the tour. Unanimous agreement.

The last show we played was at The Woods Centre, Plymouth, a date tacked onto the end of the tour. It was a great show and absolutely packed out. All the bands – The Clash, The Heartbreakers and us – played really well. The promoter loved it so much he decided to put us on again the following night.

Hardly anyone turned up. He hadn't had time to advertise it properly and obviously Plymouth is a bit light on word-of-mouth. The entire audience was six Hell's Angels and the other bands on the tour.

So we didn't even bother to get changed into our stage clothes, just played for each other. Each band passed their guitars down from the stage when they'd finished and the next lot got up and did their set.

The other highlight of Plymouth was the partying back at the hotel after the show. Not that I saw much of it. I got really sloshed and, as Sophie Richmond put it in her diary, had a 'serious conversation' with her. Then I passed out.

But during the night, while I was asleep, there was a real ruckus in the hotel. People thrown in the swimming pool, smashing up rooms, all that lark.

Two or three years later I went back there with Iggy Pop, who I was touring with at the time, playing bass. They wouldn't let us stay in the hotel, all of us were barred from it just because *I* had once been a Sex Pistol. As it was the only decent hotel in Plymouth, we had to stay in a real shit hole. But Iggy quite dug the whole thing, enjoyed the idea of notoriety and thought it was really funny.

All we seemed to do on the tour was shuttle up and down motorways in the coach and hang around hotels. Everybody thinks the 'Anarchy' tour was hey! hey! hey! But it wasn't. The main thing I remember is the boredom. We didn't know what the fuck was going on. We had no money and we were sitting around hotel rooms all the time, not playing.

To begin with it was a novelty staying in hotels and we all had a lot of fun ordering up room service. We got really silly with our orders.

An awful lot of money went down the dumper in those early days before Malcolm twigged about room service and cut it off, making us pay for our own food. After that we'd often have nothing more lavish than Bernie fetching us fish and chips.

But, in those first few days, while Malcolm was off in different towns, dealing with the press, leaving Bernie in charge, we were all steaming into room service, ordering this, that and the other.

It was all toasted cheese sarnies, triple decker club numbers with all the trimmings, bowls of crisps, beer and more beer—and while you're about it, waiter, keep it coming.

No one wanted it billed back to themselves so everyone signed for it under false names. Donald Duck was the big favourite. I remember Mick and I ordered some food and when the waitress brought the tray to our room I signed it 'Donald Duck'. Oh no, she said, not again. Can't you think of something more original than that, you're the fifteenth Donald Duck I've had today.

When we cracked up she looked at us like we were mad. But, being a Northerner, she had no idea that Donald Duck is a really obvious piece of rhyming slang.

As well as the food and booze, The Heartbreakers spent a fortune on calling their girls back home in the States and charging it to their rooms. To begin with we thought it was fair enough. Then we eventually realised that it was something else coming out of our EMI advance.

As we were covering the costs of the tour, it was *our* money, no one else's, that was being gobbled up in cheese sarnies, cans of Heineken and transatlantic phone calls. We were footing the bill for all the other bands' non-payment. Every time someone signed 'Donald Duck' they were really signing 'Jones/ Matlock/Cook/Rotten'.

We began to think, hang on, it's all very well Malcolm saying we've got to do this tour because we need the publicity but look at the money being spent – which is *all* coming out of *our* pockets.

It all added to the souring atmosphere on the tour. Not only were we bored all the time, and frustrated by not being able to play, but we also had to put up with the knowledge that, just by being out on the road, we were losing money hand over fist.

Malcolm's attitude – and I agree with it to this day – was that we couldn't just knock it on the head, turn round and go back to London. That would look like we'd been defeated by all those arseholes round the country.

So we had to stay out there, which we did. Nearly a month of hotel bills with just three gigs to show for it. But we'd still dutifully turn up for the next gig expecting – well, hoping – to play.

We partly turned up to show that we meant it and that we weren't going to be beaten back. But we also partly turned up so the promoter couldn't claim we'd goofed off and therefore he wouldn't have to pay us the half of the money he was contractually obliged to shell out.

The deal was always that if we turned up and then the gig was cancelled – for whatever reason – we had to be paid half of the money. That was the theory anyway. Whether we ever got any of that money, I've no idea. The accounts of the tour I was shown later were flimsy to say the least.

When I left the band I got a pay-off and, according to the figures I saw, there was less than £10,000 left out of the £50,000 advance EMI had given us a few months before. The 'Anarchy' tour really did eat up a lot of money but I've no idea how the final figure was arrived at.

We weren't paying the bills for The Damned but we were for the other two bands. Putting them up in five star hotels really put a big hole in our advance. And, of course, the tour established The Pistols' cred. But that was no good for me. For them it was like investing in a capital asset. For me it was a straight deduction.

On top of which I've no idea how much we were being paid for gigs and what the travelling costs and hotel bills were. There certainly weren't any details in the accounts I was given.

This financial mess also contributed to the increasingly low morale on the tour. As we sat around waiting, rather than playing, the whole party split into different factions. Even on the coach we had separate sections.

The bloke who got the absolute worst of it was The Clash's drummer, who only joined them for the tour and left straight afterwards – which made perfect sense. No one would talk to him. No one at all.

I felt sorry for him so every now and again I'd have a little chat with him. Everyone else, particularly The Clash, would say, what are you talking to *him* for?

Imagine going through an entire tour with no one talking to you. What had happened was that The Clash had somehow got it into their heads that he was a Herbert. That's what The Clash thought and he was their drummer so it became what everyone else thought as well. This drummer – who was an OK drummer and certainly fit to grace the stage with the rest of the band – became a Herbert in a whole coach-full of people's eyes.

But the splits and the factions ran right through the coach. In fact, I think it was on the 'Anarchy' tour that it began to get really difficult between me and John.

I'd hang out with Mick Jones and I think that got the rest of The Pistols' backs up. At the time it struck me as funny. It was only later that I thought about it and I realised that this ran right against what we were meant to be standing for.

By this stage we'd all come to terms with the fact that, whether we liked it or not, we were going to be called punk rockers. So we were all meant to uphold the idea of all punk rockers together as one big unit.

150

But as soon as I spoke to someone from another band the rest of them had me down as a turncoat. Make up your bloody minds, I thought.

Malcolm was particularly like that. John as well. And the funny thing was that The Clash thought of Mick as a turncoat because he was hanging out with me.

Perhaps things got difficult between me and John because we'd pretty much ceased to have any rapport. I certainly remember feeling isolated. It was hard being out there and even harder not getting on with everyone. Plus I didn't have much support from my parents. Not that I really expected any—my mum hadn't wanted anything to do with me since they'd started calling her Mrs Sex Pistol at work. I remember having a donking row with my dad over that.

One day, though, I decided to call her up and smooth things out. How's everything going? I said. Really I was looking for a bit of tea and sympathy, because it was no laugh being out there. But I sure as hell didn't get any. They felt they had enough problems of their own without taking on mine.

To be honest, I was feeling a bit ostracised by the rest of The Pistols by then, although I could never have expressed it that clearly at the time. Maybe hanging out with Mick Jones was a bad move. Maybe the reason I fell out with the rest of them is all down to Mick Jones.

Which sounds ridiculous, of course. But maybe that really was the reason. That's the way it can go. Maybe all that personality conflict became more important than what we could accomplish as a group. Perhaps it all got brought out by being on the road and holed up in hotels. That's just not like a normal experience. It's a very abnormal way of life.

When we first got back to London from the tour it wasn't too bad. It was nearly Christmas and I happened to be in the office with Malcolm when a Fortnum and Mason hamper arrived from EMI. They'd pulled our single but they still sent us a Christmas present

Me and Malcolm went through the lot before anyone else turned up—the champagne, the bottle of port, the Dundee cake. Later the others arrived. We got this great present from EMI, we told them.

Oh yeah? they said, let's have some.

Sorry, nothing left except empty bottles. Hic.

After that we did nothing, absolutely nothing. The single had been pulled; the tour had collapsed; we had no idea which way to turn or what the future might be.

It was at this time that Malcolm first started really getting into the publicity idea of himself. They can't play, he began to say, they're my boys; I do this, I do that.

Every time there was an interview it was Malcolm who was being interviewed, not us. And that wasn't what it was all about. Not for me anyway.

Then I'd go out to gigs and people would come up to me and say, Glen, we can put on The Pistols, do a big gig in Brighton, fancy it? Now, aside from The Roxy Club, who had approached us about headlining their New Year's Eve show which we'd turned down because we wanted to distance ourselves from all these new bands jumping on our bandwagon — these were real promoters and they were deadly serious. No Mickey Mouse stuff here.

So I'd speak to Malcolm and he'd say, no, no, they won't let us play there. He was soft-soaping me all along. I was getting really frustrated by all this. I was in a band and I wanted to *play*.

13

GOING Dutch

the last gigs I played with the band were two nights at The Paradiso in Amsterdam. One of us, either me or Steve, threw up at Heathrow airport on the way out – from nerves or too much to drink. But the press made a big thing about it, writing that John was the one who was sick, probably because his was the name everyone would recognise.

We actually played four shows in Holland; two in Amsterdam, one in Rotterdam and a TV show, with a dwarf. Golden Earring were also on the TV show. I met the bass player and told him I really liked his playing. He said, great, any particular song? I said, 'Radar Love', their only big British hit. And he just walked away and wouldn't talk to me again. I must have been the nineteen-hundredth person to have said that to him.

The show was in a circus tent with jugglers and this dwarf. I felt really sorry for him. The producer wanted him to stand in front of John on stage twirling a plate on a stick. None of us wanted that. A dwarf's a dwarf, but something like that had nothing to do with us. So the poor dwarf was caught between a rock and a hard place. We kept on slinging him off stage while the producer kept on trying to push him back on. During the actual live show, he had one leg up on the stage trying to get on because the producer was over the other side of the tent, gesturing fiercely at him to get on stage. Steve meanwhile was holding his guitar up in the air above him, as if to say; any further and you'll get this wrapped around your head. In the end he must have scuttled off somewhere. Whether he worked in show business again after that is a good question.

While we were there Malcolm decided I wasn't 'out there' enough on stage. At the same time he asked us all to see if we could come up with a plan to cause a bit of a stir there. John and Steve couldn't think of anything. I suggested going to one of their major monuments and daubing 'Sex Pistols' all over it. Malcolm said, yeah, let's do it. That'll really get up the noses of the Dutch. But the other guys didn't care, they didn't have a clue.

What they were interested in was prostitutes. It was all, let's go and get Glen a tart. It may sound like I was a party-pooper, but I wasn't interested. One, I had my eyes on a girl at The Paradiso. Two, I had a couple of songs to work on and one of the songs I wrote there turned out to be 'Rich Kids' which sold 100,000 copies, thank you very much. Not great but not bad. So sod going off after a tart.

We stayed in what the Amsterdamers call a brown: a café with rooms above. This particular one was run by an old couple who regularly put up bands who were playing at The Melkweg – The Milky Way – which is a smaller club than The Paradiso where our gig was. Because of the 'incident' at Heathrow the phone kept going for us. The old couple were quite taken aback by this because they were only used to these scuzzy little bands who no one wanted to talk to.

One morning I staggered down rather bleary-eyed for breakfast and the old woman said, Glen, it's the *Daily Mirror* on the phone for you. So the next thing I heard was this voice telling me, you've been sacked from EMI. How do you feel about it? I said, well that's nice isn't it? I meant it ironically but, as it was the very first thing I'd said to anyone that morning, maybe it didn't come out sounding that way. Of course, it came out in the papers as: Glen Matlock thinks it's really nice that The Sex Pistols have been dumped by EMI. The rest of the band really gave me a hard time over that.

But it was odd that EMI chose that time to get rid of us. Leslie Hill, one of the big guys from the EMI London office, was over there with us–staying in a big flash hotel while we were in this little café. He'd try and keep us occupied. It was as if the airport incident had been set up deliberately to disgrace us, with EMI working in collusion with KLM, the Dutch airline.

It seemed long after the Grundy thing. That show had gone out right at the beginning of December 1976 and we didn't go to Amsterdam until the beginning of 1977. Maybe it had taken things that long to reach fever pitch at EMI or maybe the people upstairs had only just woken up to what had been going on. Whatever the truth, it felt like a real dirty trick, sacking us while we were out of the country on the back of a non-existent incident at Heathrow.

It was also a really testing time for me. I'd basically had enough by then. John was acting up dreadfully. At the end of the second show at The Paradiso I walked straight off stage and refused to go back on and do an encore. I was just fed up with being in the same place as John.

He was totally conceited, arrogant and stroppy just for the sake of it. He would say things which he obviously knew were bloody stupid just to get a reaction, purely to get someone's back up. Which is fine once in a while but with him it was all the bloody time. I didn't need it. I thought, this is stupid, I've had enough, I've really had enough. I flew back to London and that was it.

We had a meeting at Food For Thought, the vegetarian café in Covent Garden–me, Paul and Steve and Malcolm. Malcolm drank his cup of tea and then said to me, what do you really think of John?

I knew there were two things I could say. Either, he's alright, I'll put up with him, or what I really felt. So I said what I felt. I can't stand him. Actually I kind of like him in a way but I can't work with somebody like that. I just can't be in the same room as him all the time. Everything has become so petty and it's dragging me down to the same level. I don't need it.

As I was talking I could see Steve and Paul's expressions. Here we bloody go, they were thinking. I think they felt the same way I did but they had a much healthier attitude to it all. They took it all with a pinch of salt. They seemed quite willing to hand over the reins of the band to John. Which was funny because it had been their band in the first place. It was almost as if there had been a corporate take-over of their company without their even realising it had happened.

Whereas I was unhappy about that. Although I like being in control as much as anybody else, I didn't in fact want to rule the roost in the band, but what I did object to was a total shift in the balance of power.

This change in the band from a democracy to John in charge all the time started happening as soon as we got press. Right from the beginning John was getting all the press attention, everything was focused on 'Johnny Rotten The Punk'. Which was fair enough, I could handle that, because singers always get most of the attention.

But what I didn't like was this: because he was always in the press, what he had to say then became so much more important – whether it was right or wrong. That really annoyed me. What counted was not whether what he was saying was right or wrong but the fact that *he* was saying it. And I didn't like that.

Steve and Paul, on the other hand, were just along for the ride by then. Their whole attitude was: it's a laugh. What must have gone through their minds as I was saying how I couldn't stand John must have been something like: it's got to be either John or Glen and John's getting all the press so goodbye, Glen. Quite honestly, it didn't bother me that much because I was already getting The Rich Kids together and – ironically – EMI had started to make overtures towards signing us.

Malcolm's attitude, however, disappointed me. Before, his attitude had always been that a band should stick together. Look at The Rolling Stones, he'd say, they've only done so well because they've stuck together all these years. Which is true and which is also shown by the example of The Clash. They became the premier punk band by default because they were the only ones who stuck together and saw it through. Well, a lot further anyway.

Yet, although Malcolm saw the wisdom of that, he also played this whole game of divide and conquer. So, rather than discourage Steve and Paul from getting on my case because I was pissed off with John, he actively encouraged them.

Those things didn't quite equate. On the one hand he wanted to keep the band together. On the other he wanted to create all these internal wranglings. In fact, it was like a smokescreen for what he was really up to. I didn't see it clearly at the time – and I don't think Malcolm did either – but in fact he wished he was the singer. Look at the way he was always winding John up about being some kind of underwater Ziggy. On the surface it was just a joke about John's red hair and 'Submission' but there was a depth to it as well, an undercurrent of Malcolm being up to something.

At the end of the meeting I felt that I'd said what I had to say and couldn't go back on it. Paul and Steve were away to the Canaries or somewhere. The girls are all topless there, they kept saying. Malcolm said, I don't know what it's all coming to, and went off to the States, presumably to peddle the tapes we'd done just after the previous Christmas at Gooseberry Studios. I just piddled around a bit, mulling things over.

Then Steve and Paul came back and started rehearsing with Sid. Although I had no intention of playing with them again, I was still hanging in there because I was getting my flat paid for, plus £25 a week. Although I'd started getting The Rich Kids together I wasn't quite sure about it all.

When Malcolm returned from the States he called me up and told me that they'd been rehearsing with Sid. I said, look, it really doesn't bother me. If they want I'll give Sid some bass lessons. Malcolm said, let's have a meeting.

So, in late February 1977, we met in The Blue Posts, a pub behind The 100 Club and had a long discussion.

Aren't you annoyed about them rehearsing with Sid? he said.

No, not really, Malcolm. I've had enough.

Then he started to give me the lecture about The Rolling Stones and went on: Glen, I want you to be strong. I want you to go back there and kick that door down and prove that the job is yours and . . .

I said, Malcolm, I'm just not interested any more. I can't be bothered with that bloke's attitude. And I can't be bothered if they're rehearsing with someone else behind my back. I don't think it's on. I knew about it already and, although I don't actually care, they should have said something to me. So let's leave it at that.

Yeah, he said, I suppose so if that's your decision.

Look, I said, if there's any way I can help out, great. I don't see why there should be any animosity. It's come to a natural split. You lot can go off and do what you want. But I don't like the way things are going. I don't like the fact that we are beginning to be seen as puppets at your beck and call – that's why I said on leaving that being in The Pistols had been like being in The Monkees.

Although I didn't say it to his face – and probably should have done – I was also thinking that he was in fact quite deliberately perpetrating that idea of us as his puppets. I realised this at the time but for some strange reason it took John an entire year and the Ronnie Biggs fiasco to latch on to this basic point. However, on the other hand, I've since found out that even Malcolm wasn't as aware of what he was up to as he has made out.

So after I'd had my say, he said, OK, fine, if that's your attitude. Shake hands and we'll leave it at that. He told me that they were going to do some recording – obviously for A&M, although he didn't say anything to me about that at the time – and asked me if I would help out because Sid wasn't too good. I agreed. When we parted his whole attitude was: great, good luck to you, it's good that we can part on these terms, it's a shame but that's the way it is.

But he also soft-soaped me into not telling anyone that I'd left the band. Then a couple of days after that meeting in The Blue Posts Mick Jones called me up and said, what are you doing tonight? Fancy coming down The Marquee?

OK, but why?

It's your going away party, leaving The Pistols and all that.

He and Joe were seriously thinking of asking me to join The Clash instead of Simonon. Which made sense because much as I like Paul he's not the best bass player in the world. But, of course, dickhead Matlock told them nothing. No, it's not definite between me and the rest of the band yet. I was just trying to help Malcolm out and keep it all sweet. Then he went and did the dirty on me.

Three days later he sent a telegram to the *NME* saying I'd been sacked because I liked The Beatles, that Sid was my replacement and that was a jolly good thing because Sid was such a hard man – he'd whacked Nick Kent, the *NME* journalist, and that was what Nick deserved. He just totally turned the truth around. It was like something out of George Orwell's *1984*, rewriting history as he went along.

I'd had enough of the band so why couldn't Malcolm just say that? The reason was simple: if he'd told the truth it would have looked like he wasn't in control and he was desperate for it to look like he was in total control. And it's been like that with him ever since. From that moment on Malcolm went right down in my estimation.

A few days later I went down to Denmark Street to pick up my gear. There was a row over whether I could have my bass cabinet back which ended with me taking it away. As I was packing everything into my car outside in the street I said, well, good luck to everybody then. Paul went, oh yeah. Malcolm said, good luck. And that was it. None of them had the bottle to say anything more to my face. And I hadn't spoken to John since Amsterdam.

But I was still going into the office to pick up my wages. There was an awkward atmosphere in there but I thought, fuck that, I've got to live. All the time I was sorting out the accounts of what money was due.

Finally I had a meeting with Sophie who looked after everything in the office. She showed me the accounts and all there was was one-and-a-half pages of writing in ballpoint. This was meant to be the complete accounting on the £50,000 advance from EMI – which doesn't even include the money we earned from gigging. At the bottom of these 'accounts' was the final figure of £2965. That was what they'd worked out as being owed to me.

One thing I didn't dispute was the agreement that all the songs should be split four ways. When it was first discussed I'd voted against it but I'd been outvoted and I'd agreed to abide by their decision. In some ways it came out in the wash. 'No Feelings' has my name on it but it's nearly all Steve's music and John's lyrics; I had very little to do with it. On the other hand, I was responsible for a major part of all the first three singles. 'Anarchy' is all my music with John's lyrics. As is 'God Save The Queen'. And 'Pretty Vacant' is entirely mine, apart from John's update of the second verse – which as I've said earlier was far better than the original. But everything else was mine.

But the figures were very peculiar. There were things like 'Sundries – £15,000' and 'Expenses – £30,000' with no more details than that. Crazy. And although I wouldn't dispute that a lot of money was lost on the 'Anarchy' tour, the amount I was getting still seemed ludicrously low.

So I had a word with Malcolm. He had a cheque there for the money that *he* reckoned I was owed. I was thinking, that's the end of my wages and I've got my flat to pay for. At the same time he was waving a cheque for nearly three grand in front of my face, which doesn't sound like a lot in 1991, but seemed slightly more reasonable then. But even so, I said, I want to see somebody about this.

Take it or leave it, he said. If you don't take it now you'll get nothing. I was young. I didn't know what the legal position was. So I thought, fuck it, I'll have to sign it. Which I did. Crazy.

That night I went down to The Nashville for a drink. I was standing quietly tucking into my drink and watching the band – Rockpile with Nick Lowe and Dave Edmunds – when a good looking American girl came up and asked if I was a Sex Pistol. I knew I should really say no, but she was such a good looking woman and I had only left that day so it was only *technically* that I wasn't a Sex Pistol. I told her I was.

Do you want to come outside with me?

Sure, I said.

You come outside with me, she said, and I'll fight you.

What?

I mean it, she said.

In that case, if it's all the same to you, I think I'll stay in here and watch the band. She started trying to have a go at me but I managed to ignore her.

Then Jake Riviera, who managed Rockpile as well as The Damned, came over. Hello Glen, what's going on here? I told him about the girl trying to get me to come outside and fight her.

He fixed my eye. So my boiler's just asked you out for a fight has she? he said, and immediately started lashing out at me. He was pissed out of his head and still trying to stir up trouble with Malcolm. Going all that way to set me up – he must have had one hell of an obsession about Malcolm. I felt that there were very few groups around who were getting something worthwhile together and that the few of us who were should look out for each other.

But, because of Malcolm, I ended up in a punch-up with Jake the very night I left The Pistols. I wasn't one of the band any more but I was still fighting their battles.

Mark Zermatti, the Frenchman who promoted the punk festivals at Mont de Marsan, was there as well. Glen, why is there this fighting between you and Jake? It is stupid. You are both on ze same side. This is a war we have to fight together, not with each other.

Tell Jake that, I said. And Malcolm.

14

Sid

after I left, the band became just what Malcolm thought they should. They were The Sex Pistols as a cartoon strip. A band of caricatures where it doesn't really matter who's in the band or who plays what. Which isn't the truth, of course. If Malcolm really thought for one second about why The Pistols' status and legacy is so great, with people still writing and thinking about them, he'd realise that the cartoon strip idea is so much garbage.

The idea of The Pistols has lasted so long because of the band's strength of character. It was a real triumph of content over style. The Pistols were so much more than just another Joe Meek/Larry Parnes-style package. They weren't just another offering from the man who sold the Eiffel Tower twice.

But that's the way Malcolm likes to pitch it. And Sid being brought into the band is the obvious example of that. Even at the time Malcolm knew full well Sid couldn't play at all.

None of the band realised the long-term effect that would have. John was happy to have Sid in the band because Sid was his mate. Instead of him against Steve and Paul, it would become him and Sid against Steve and Paul. He always thought of it in terms of opposing camps and he always had to have his camp allied with him.

Now with Sid on my side, he thought, plus the fact that I'm cleverer than Steve and Paul, I'll certainly win. But, of course, it didn't work out that way.

Steve and Paul, I don't think they thought it through at all. Not even Sid not being able to play. John easily swallowed Malcolm's line about how musical ability was irrelevant because he was only a vocalist and couldn't play anything anyway. But Steve and Paul also fell for that line – which is a pity because they could play well, and by accepting Malcolm's view they were decrying their own talent.

In fact, despite what a lot of other people might think, I always felt I got on fine with Sid. Shortly after he got the OK to join the band I bumped into him in The Roxy.

How you getting on with the bass? I asked.

Bit slow.

So I offered to give him some lessons.

Really?

I don't see why not, I said.

Aren't you pissed off that I'm in the band instead of you?

No, I said, not particularly. I'd had enough. Give me a call if you want some help on the bass. But he never called.

I didn't see him again till maybe a year later when I saw him in The Warrington, a pub in Maida Vale, where both he and I lived at the time.

What's all this, he said, about people not thinking we're mates. We're mates aren't we?

Of course, Sid, we get on alright don't we?

Yeah, course we do. So what are we gonna do about all these people thinking we don't? He thought a bit. Then he said, we could do a gig.

I was up for that.

Great.

I'm going to America soon, you know. This is the last time I'll be in England. I'll be dead by the time I'm 21.

Sid, that really is a fine thing to say when you're trying to have a quiet drink with someone. But, this gig. If you're really up for it, I'll get a band together.

Who? Scabies on drums, I suggested. I like Scabies, he said. Good drummer. He hits them hard. Steve New on guitar? I like Steve, he said. One thing, though, if you're a bass player and I'm a bass player—who's going to play bass? Well, let me put it this way, Sid, I'm certainly not going to sing. Who's going to sing then? How about you sing and I play bass? Oh yeah, he said, I get it. So we did a show together. We called ourselves The Vicious White Kids, on account of how it was an amalgamation of all our names. Steve New and I were in The Rich Kids. Scabies at that time had a band called The White Cats. And Sid was Sid.

We rehearsed at EZee Hire in Islington. When we walked into the room there was nothing in it but some old PA cabinets. Then we noticed a brand new Fender Mustang bass propped up against a wall in the corner. Cor, look at that, said Sid. I'm having that for my honey. Meaning Nancy, of course. So he nicked it. But to get it out to the car he had to walk through the yard. And the offices were in a porta-cabin in the yard, a portacabin with enormous windows. He trooped through with this big, brand new bass in his hand. The EZee Hire people must have been sitting there watching him, thinking: this looks like a right laugh, why don't we let him go through with it now, we can pull him up later. So we went on with the rehearsal as if nothing had happened. At the end of it Sid turned to me and said, I can't believe it, Glen, you can play a bass guitar all the way through a song without stopping.

Well, I thought, there you go.

I must admit I was a bit anxious about Sid nicking the bass but I didn't think much more about it till the next day—which was the day of the show. Late afternoon. I got a call from our roadie, Henry McGroggan. He'd gone over to EZee Hire to pick up our gear. Here Glen, he said, we've got problems here. They won't let us have the gear on account of something to do with a Fender Mustang bass guitar.

So I scooted right over there. I tried to deny all knowledge of it. But they didn't want to know. And how could I convince them when it was so bloody obvious that Sid was the phantom Mustang grabber?

Then Sid turned up. He swore blind he hadn't nicked it. He was absolutely, totally, completely believable. I would have believed him myself if I hadn't seen him nick it. And, of course, the rest of them had seen him lift it too.

I took him to one side and said, Sid, look, if we don't get the bass back, they won't give us the gear back. And if we don't get the gear back we won't be able to do the gig. And if we have to cancel the gig you won't get the money. And if you don't have any money . . .

So I got him to phone Nancy and she put the bass in a cab and sent it round. We were running late so I asked the bloke from EZee Hire if we could load up our gear while we were waiting. As soon as the bass turns up, we can shoot straight off, OK?

OK.

All the gear was stacked in the van and we waited for the cab. When it turned up the cabbie just reached out and handed the EZee Hire bloke the bass wrapped in a black plastic bin liner – very punk – and drove off.

As we did. Looking back we could see him take it out of the bin bag. It was dripping paint, matt black paint. Nancy must have taken it into her head to paint it that afternoon.

By the look of it she couldn't have painted it long before Sid called to tell her to put it in the cab. It looked dreadful. She hadn't bothered to take the strings off before painting it and she must have used a four-inch brush to slosh it on. The bloke just stood there staring at his beautiful, spanking new Fender Mustang bass guitar, watching the paint drip off the fretboard, onto his hand and, splosh, onto the floor.

We waved goodbye as we drove off.

The gig itself was good. We were the second lot of ex-Pistols to play the same hall, The Electric Ballroom in Camden Town, within a week. The previous Thursday Steve and Paul had played there with Phil Lynott from Thin Lizzy. They

called themselves The Greedy Bastards. Theirs was the co-
caine night. Ours was the booze and smack night.

I really enjoyed playing–even though I was pissed out of
my head and we did the same set of songs three times in a row.
We played The Stooges' 'Search And Destroy' and The
Monkees' 'Steppin' Stone'. And we did 'My Way', which Sid
wasn't at all keen on singing, and a few other so-called punk
rock anthems. In fact, I reckon we would have made a good
permanent group.

Nancy was funny, though. She insisted on being on stage
right through the show, and singing–which was not the most
melodious of noises. When I heard her bleating away at the
soundcheck I was really worried about it. I had a word with
Henry. Don't worry, he said, I had no intention of turning her
mike on.

Actually I used to see a lot of her, much more than Sid. She
was always round at my flat. She'd come round to the flat to
get my girlfriend, Celia, to take her Levis out. She was always
getting fatter. She seemed to put on weight as you looked at
her.

Every now and again Celia would try and explain tactfully
to her that there was only so much fabric in the back of a pair
of jeans. You couldn't let them out forever. As it was, the arse
looked like a sergeant's stripes with all the lines of different
coloured denim where it had faded unevenly.

Nancy was a total pain. One time I came in and she was
sitting in my kitchen with her wrists slashed, dripping blood
into a plastic bowl while eating ice cream. (And ice cream, of
course, is why Miss Fat Arse always needed her jeans taken
out.)

What *are* you up to, I said.

I cut my wrists. Sid doesn't love me any more. And she's
still sitting there eating the ice cream. I thought, I don't need
this fucking stupid play-acting, and went to the pub.

I could never work Sid out. A lot of people thought he was
stupid, but he wasn't. He was very intelligent but talked like

he wasn't. He just wasn't very articulate. Personally, I could never work out what he was so unhappy about.

Strangely enough, I didn't really get to know him till after he joined The Pistols. Before that he was just one of John's entourage. He'd come to all our gigs and he'd come into the shop now and again. And he'd wear those horrible jelly shoes, just like John.

The first real memory I have of him is when I was still working in Malcolm's shop. I knew he was going out with a girl that I'd been going out with. She must have had a thing about bass players.

It was Saturday afternoon and Bernie came bounding into the shop. Cor, he said, that Sid's a one, he must be mad.

Why?

I was standing there, he said, talking to Vivienne – not Westwood but Albertine, later she was in The Slits – and Sid, when this middle-aged woman came up – the mother of the girl you used to go out with. She doesn't like Sid going out with her daughter. She came up to us and was about to have a pop at Sid when he whipped his dick out and said, get a load of that, missus.

Bernie was really impressed. You've got to have a lot of bottle to do something like that in broad daylight, you know. Vivienne Westwood said something stupid as usual. It is hot, she said naively and in all seriousness. Maybe it needed airing.

Stupid as it sounds, Sid really was on some kind of death trip. He was always saying it himself. I'm not going to live past 21, he'd say.

Yet, when you think about it, he had it all going for him. He was the bass player in the most notorious band in the world, yet he didn't even have to get it together to learn how to play the bass properly. But it all went wrong. That's heroin for you.

I'm occasionally asked if it annoys me that Sid is more famous in death than I've ever been in my life. The answer is well, yes – because sometimes, just once in a while, I get to thinking why is it that so many lost souls become so fascinated by those who live their lives so close to the edge that they end up falling off? Too fast to live, too young to die? The cult of James Dean, the continuing fascination with digging out the real story behind the death of Marilyn Monroe and poor old Sid. In reality these people are the losers. They're the party-poopers.

15

Glorious
HINDSIGHT

these people, they're worse than the Gestapo, said my Jewish accountant as we walked through the portals of Bush House in the Aldwych. He seemed to mean it too. He was pouring sweat and I could see his eyes flickering worriedly behind his thick spectacles.

This is the special office in the Inland Revenue, he said. You must watch *everything* you say. They're completely ruthless.

Quite simply, it was down to Malcolm that I was there. He'd put all those money stories about, the ones that were big on taking record companies for rides and stuffing dosh into The Sex Pistols' coffers.

So I was summoned to appear before the Inland Revenue's special office which had been set up to deal expressly with rock bands. They'd heard Malcolm's stories, they'd checked out the charts – where The Pistols' singles were riding high – and they'd called me in to demand their pound of flesh.

At that particular moment I didn't have as much as an ounce to give them. I was broke. The money I'd got on leaving The Pistols had gone. I'd still to sign The Rich Kids to EMI and my publishing deal was still being sorted out. I was living in a squat in Stoke Newington. All I knew was that I was due some money at some point in the future. Mostly, though, I was dining on hope.

But even my accountant didn't believe me. He was quite obviously convinced that I was lying and was tucking the money away somewhere. He clearly thought I'd go into this meeting and let the cat out of the bag. Resigned terror would be a fair description of his mood.

So up the stairs I went. I remember the wood panelling, the pictures and drawings by Winston Churchill on the wall and thinking: these paintings are worth a few bob, they might not be the greatest works of art but why do they need to put them here, tucked out of the general public's view?

The meeting room was dominated by a table – a big oval thing that must have been 20 feet long. We sat at one end. They sat at the other.

They were the tax officer and his sidekick, the Batman and Robin of the Inland Revenue's rock band department. Batman fired the questions. Robin didn't say a word, just wrote down every answer laboriously and carefully. Every now and then they'd look at each other, nod, mumble and write a little more.

Right, they said, what's happened to all the money.

What money?

The money you got from Malcolm McLaren.

Well, it wasn't a fortune.

Well, he said, maybe it wasn't a fortune to you. It all depends on what you call a fortune, doesn't it? So how much was it exactly?

Exactly seven pounds.

Seven pounds?

Seven pounds a day exactly all the time I was his Saturday lad. Okay, maybe I'm getting him into a bit of trouble by saying that because it's possible he didn't pay my tax and stamp and all that but . . .

Seven pounds?

Well, yeah, plus 25 pounds a week later on when we'd signed to EMI.

Are you sure?

Absolutely. I think you're barking up the wrong tree.

All through this my accountant looked a deeply worried man. He was wringing his hands to keep the sweat from dripping onto his lap. He thought I was lying.

But I wasn't. I was telling the truth and had nothing to hide so I must have been quite convincing. Whatever, I never heard from them again.

The whole episode was a real eye-opener, though. The band had tried to strike out and create something fresh and there was all this furor, with people in high places denouncing us as evil. Yet suddenly, come accounting time, they didn't half want their money double quick. I was really peeved. They'd spent most of that winter trying to stop us earning a living and now they wanted their share of it. It also showed that people in high places were paying attention to Malcolm's spiel.

There was that political edge to the band which really did seem to twist the tails of our masters. We *were* a challenge to the government's absolute power.

Our politics were clear in 'Anarchy'. We weren't political in the sense of saying: be a Socialist, be a Tory, be a Communist. We were political in the sense that we didn't even entertain the idea of politics, it was below us.

It was anarchy in its purest sense: self-determination. We couldn't, we felt, do much about changing the system but we weren't going to let the system do anything to us. We wanted to live our lives how we wanted to live them – and we went out and did it.

Which is a necessary ingredient of being an 'out there' rock person. The Stones had that philosophy in the early days, and Jerry Lee Lewis has lived his entire life by that creed.

When The Clash started doing all their political songs we were happy to let them do it; we weren't interested. As a lyricist John was always more Dostoevsky than Tariq Ali. He was just generally right out there on a limb, sending up notes from beneath his own floorboards.

He was an extraordinarily self-centred man. All his songs

were about himself and his own personality problems and his conflicts with other people. He lived in a bubble of his own.

But, although he was wrapped up in himself, other people could latch onto his songs because we all have those same feelings. He had no monopoly on teenage angst—maybe just a little more of it than some people. His lyrics tapped the collective consciousness and caught the speed of the moment.

But we never wanted to make big political statements. When John said 'Liar' was about Harold Wilson, that was about as political as we ever got. For us, being in a band *was* our politics. We didn't want to be straight and boring. We didn't want to lead nine to five lives. We wanted to be in a band.

As my dad was a lifelong trade unionist, I was the most politically-minded of us but if I so much as mentioned something I would get very short shrift indeed. Not that I knew much about the larger world anyway. My only real experience of how people lived—and how much money they had in their pockets—was my own family and the holiday jobs I did.

Our dissatisfaction had nothing to do with keeping up with the Joneses. Apart from Malcolm, I just didn't know anyone who could afford to hang out at places like Biba's nightclub, drinking pina coladas. And the same went for the rest of the band. That just wasn't part of our world.

Being in a band *was* our world. Paul had a job but that was nothing more than a chance to put some money in his pocket. Being an electrician for the rest of his life was hardly his idea of a good time. Steve never wanted to work. He was happy being a thief. If somebody gave him a job as a stockbroker he'd have nicked the computer by lunchtime and been off with a secretary by the time the elevens came round. It was Steve, not John or Sid, who was the real spirit behind The Sex Pistols. He was the one who did whatever he liked whenever he liked—something that most people don't have the honesty or guts to do. Perhaps he was just plain dumb, but you couldn't help but admire the fact that he was the one who really didn't give a shit.

I had my artistic pretensions and had no intention of being behind a desk all day long. And John. Can you imagine John doing a job? It's quite amusing to imagine what might have happened to John if he hadn't chanced across us. His mum, I think, was quite pleased with us for taking him off her hands.

When Gene October and Chelsea came up with that song, 'Right To Work', we couldn't believe it. It was a complete joke. Gene October had never done a day's work in his life and had no desire to—not even so much as a stroke. That was a case of finding a topic that his audience could identify with and adding his own slant to it. John didn't need to carry on like that. He had his own thing going.

I think overtly political songs like that are a fast road to nowhere. I think it's decidedly grim when kids listen to—and are swayed by—kids not much older than themselves. Rock stars being what they are, they stick loads of gear up their noses. So there they are preaching about their political persuasions and how an ideal world should be arranged when all along they're deeply fucked up themselves. It's just intrinsically *wrong*.

The other big thing I learned at the Inland Revenue's rock 'n' roll Star Chamber was how important money is as an arbiter of success. In anything where money is involved the only real acid test of how well you are doing is how much money you scoop up. Money is the yardstick by which you measure what you've achieved and what you haven't. Whatever walk of life you're in, money is clout. Not artistic integrity. (I know a lot of people would say there was no artistic integrity in The Sex Pistols but, obviously, I would disagree.)

Our intention was to be up there with The Stones and all those other big bands. And, at one stage, we really had them on the run. Us and The Clash declaring: no Elvis, Beatles or Rolling Stones in 1977. Mick Jagger must have been wetting his knickers. Yet he's still here and we're not. He's still around because of the respect he has engendered in the business and the establishment. He can get things done because people only take notice if you've got money to wave in front of them. And he has the money to wave.

Being realistic, The Sex Pistols were a total failure. And if they really though about it – doing some honest soul searching – John, Paul and Steve would have to agree with me. We had so much going for us – our originality, our freshness, our songs, our ideas, the fact that we could play, despite what anyone might say – yet we blew it. It was like a case of premature ejaculation. Over in a flash, and deeply unsatisfying.

We created a lot of talk and a lot of pie-in-the-sky theorising, but what was the end result of it all? When you cut right to the chase, The Pistols – and the whole punk phenomenon – were an inoculation for the music business which has enabled it to survive in its current depressingly flat state.

Get a typhoid shot and you don't feel too well for a day or so but, if and when the big attack comes along, your body is ready to resist. That's what The Pistols did for the music business. We thought we had them but we didn't. As soon as the weakness was exposed they put the doors straight down. And we were no longer around to bash them open again.

Now, in the 1990s, the music business is even straighter than it was in the late fifties and early sixties. Then it was Larry Parnes and Joe Meek. The old style music publishers of Tin Pan Alley were in their heyday, running things and turning out music that was safe, whitewashed and clean, no threat to anybody.

And we're back to that. There are a few indie bands who are trying, but they just don't have the clout to make it count. They're nothing more than a sidetrack for kids who then end up being pigeonholed and compartmentalised. It's an army with very few soldiers and no capacity for taking the high ground.

It's also a sidetrack which totally suits the music business's aim of keeping control. With little valves like that to let off steam, the music business controls the important areas.

Which is totally the reverse of what we set out to achieve. When we started playing it was the first time in years that kids had any real control of their own music. The music was actually coming from them, not being foisted upon them.

So why did The Pistols peter out as unimpressively as they did?

Naïvety played a major part as did internal wranglings. The common cause got lost amid the power struggles. And I certainly feel guilty for letting those struggles get on top of me.

But I think a lot of the blame must be laid at Malcolm's feet. He should have known better than to have carried on his divide-and-conquer tactics and realised the strength of having a tight unit.

The turning point came the day after the Bill Grundy show. Up till that moment Malcolm thought of himself as the band's manager, no more, no less. But that morning, in his office, he realised all the national papers were calling *him*.

For the first time in his life he was in a position of real consequence. No longer was he just a shmutter merchant or an outlandish art student, someone of whom people would say, he's a one, watch him, he's a bit fly. Suddenly he had some real power at last. But what he did with that power was minimal. Look at the movie, *The Great Rock 'n' Roll Swindle*. It's absolute tripe and its version of The Pistols' story is pure fabrication. And Steve should be ashamed of himself for portraying the Philip Marlowe gumshoe in the movie, thereby abetting Malcolm in perpetuating his scam. It showed a total lack of self-respect on his part.

The Pistols have become one of history's big So What?'s. Partly because a lot of people—the music business most obviously—have an interest in seeing that nothing like that ever happens again. For a while we really had the record companies running from pillar to post. They didn't know what in hell was going on. They were beside themselves with desperation.

Take the example of Chris Parry, Polydor Records A&R man. Malcolm had led him to believe that he could sign us and never bothered to tell him we'd gone with EMI. He found out when he met us on our way out of a recording session – paid for by Polydor – at Kingsbury Studios in Holborn. He just broke down and cried in the middle of the street. He was desperate to get a piece of the action. He had to have his punk band otherwise history would leave him on the dung heap. The Clash pulled the same stunt and ultimately he ended up with The Jam – some consolation.

Malcolm's a cunt, he kept saying between bursts of tears.

So, we said, you only just found out? And left him there sobbing.

Like every A&R man, he was somebody with a lot of power over other people's lives. He could decide whether or not to sign someone. On his word a lot of money would be pumped in to make someone a success and set them up for the rest of their lives. That's power.

It's not the power to move armies but it's the power to affect people in a profound way. It's on a par with being the person in charge of grants at a college. So many scholarships are handed out each year and somebody decides who gets them. And who doesn't. That's going to affect you for the rest of your life.

The record companies were in a quandary. They thought the music was horrible but they *had* to get a piece of that action. They didn't know what they were doing or why but they knew something was happening and they had to have a hunk of it.

So who ultimately profited most from The Sex Pistols?

There is a simple two-word answer. Richard Branson. And an explanation to go with it. Till The Pistols came along, Virgin Records was a few shops and a label full of talentless hippies who were selling a decreasing number of records on the strength of their wishy-washy 'alternative' ideals. The Pistols made Virgin hip, gave Branson access to the mainstream and laid the foundation stone for the massive expansion of his Moonie-ish empire during the eighties.

As well as giving Branson a massive kick in the right direction, The Pistols also paved the way for a load of no-hope bands who jumped on the bandwagon to enjoy their 15 minutes of fame.

Malcolm also did well out of the band, building his career on our backs. For example, four years after the band split up, Malcolm put a rumour around town that we were going to get back together again. There was no truth in that whatsoever. John, for one, wouldn't give him the steam off his piss. And I don't think I would either. But his real reason for putting that rumour around was to get attention for himself. Of course, he did do a certain amount of things for the band. But he didn't do everything. What he never realised was that we were a unit.

The Pistols were – as Bernard Rhodes put it to me – Steve, Paul, Glen, John and *then* Malcolm. *In that order.*

But Malcolm never believed that. He always believes what he wants to believe. The Stones or The Who were a gang of people. Malcolm never gave that idea the time of day. If he's so clever what's he done since? What has he done that is of real worth?

Recently I was thinking about what Malcolm had brought to the world. In the movie he says, I brought you this and I brought you that. Yet, when you come right down to it, apart from making a few comedy records, I think the main thing he brought the world is peg trousers. Which is no shameful achievement. Peg trousers are peg trousers. But they are a total sideline to what he set out to achieve. Still, lots of great achievements are sidelines. Penicillin, for example. And peg trousers.

Did I do the right thing in leaving the band? No. I did totally the wrong thing. I was very selfish. I should have stuck in there. Not for financial reasons – because although they would have come into it, it wasn't even on my mind at the time – but because if you start something, you should see the job through.

However, at that stage, I didn't realise that for a rock band seeing a job through is breaking America. You have to crack America to have real clout. Once you've done that, you've really achieved something. It's all well and good being a household name in England, but it doesn't really count for much in the big world. I remember going to Australia and being treated like some little specimen. I was on the same level as a channel swimmer or a circus dwarf.

And I think The Pistols could have conquered the States if I'd stayed in the group. One thing the Americans do respect is a good rocking unit. (And they're prepared to pay heavy cash for it. In late 1988 one of the biggest American booking agencies offered a guarantee of 12 million dollars for a reformed Pistols tour. John turned it down to tour with New Order—which must have been something of a humble pie dinner for him. Johnny Rotten, who started the whole punk movement, supporting somebody as crummy as New Order?)

As long as I was in the band we were a solid unit. With Sid they weren't. As a band they were distinctly one sandwich short of a picnic. That again was down to Malcolm. He decided he could do it all himself. While I was there I'd argue with him and actually win quite a lot. There are always lots of opinions around. It would be wonderful if you always got your own way because you were always right. But nobody ever is.

You need a diversity of ideas and thoughts. You need a filtering process which dumps the bad ones and only lets the good ones through. And you can only get that with a bunch of people who bring a breadth of different interests into any situation. You need a team. And we had a team. But we lost sight of what this entails—teamwork.

Malcolm made one major mistake. If he was going to have a cartoon strip type of band he should never have let them tour. They should have made albums and chaotic guest appearances on the Carson show. But they should never have played live because they just couldn't cut it. The only way they could have cut it live was with me in the band because I was the one who understood *and* saw the whole picture of what we could achieve musically. And I'd already gone—as a direct consequence of Malcolm's machinations. A complete lack of foresight on his part.

People often ask me if The Pistols are an albatross round my neck. And yes, they are. As a musician I've got into different types of music with The Rich Kids, The Spectres and Iggy Pop—but people always expect me to be a Sex Pistol and play that kind of music. Lately, though, I don't see that as such an albatross as I used to. I've dabbled in all different kinds of things but now I think I'm coming back to that real basic rock that I started out with.

If you can do just one thing really well in this life, then that's good enough. It makes you square up to what your role is in the scheme of things. Simple as that.

So, my last word on The Sex Pistols? Well, just before we signed to EMI—before the rot set in—it was that one-to-one situation of playing *live* music before a *live* audience. This is the period cited by people such as Adam Ant, Morrissey and Billy Idol as one of their greatest influences—The Pistols in '76. Yesterday I was a crud, said Joe Strummer after seeing us at The Nashville on April 3, 1976, today I'm a king.

So, if you were one of those fortunate few, one of the hundreds who did witness the band live—as opposed to the thousands who claim they did—you'd understand what all the fuss was about and I'm sure you could only agree with me. We were fucking great.